JOAQUÍN ROD

Voice & Vis

JOAQUÍN RODRIGO
Voice & Vision

Selected Writings on Music

Translated by

Raymond Calcraft and Elizabeth Matthews

I

Composers and their Music

Rodrigo on his own Music

2016

Published by CMC and under licence
by Brown Dog Books
7 Green Park Station, Bath BA1 1JB

ISBN printed book: 978-1-78545-082-2
ISBN e-book: 978-1-78545-083-9

Cover design by Kevin Rylands

Printed and bound by
CPI Group (UK) Ltd, Croydon CR0 4YY

for Cecilia

rubí en caridad, en fe diamante

JOAQUÍN RODRIGO
Voice & Vision

CONTENTS

Acknowledgements

All the writings by Joaquín Rodrigo translated here are taken from material held in the archives of the Victoria and Joaquín Rodrigo Foundation in Madrid. We are very grateful to the composer's daughter, Cecilia, for providing us with access to many areas of her father's life, his music and his writings, critical works on the composer, and a wealth of material garnered from decades of newspaper articles and interviews, all faithfully preserved at the Foundation's offices. Several members of Countess Cecilia's staff have offered generous help to us in our work, in particular Paula Lorenzo and Carmen Santás, responsible respectively for archiving and computer records. The images and photographs in the book are reproduced by courtesy of the Rodrigo Foundation, apart from the dual portrait of Joaquín and Victoria Rodrigo, taken in 1986 by Robert Royal, to whom we express our grateful thanks. Our agent, Francesca White, and several colleagues at Brown Dog Books in Bath have all offered valuable advice and help during the preparation of this book. We are also greatly indebted to Gabriel Woolf for undertaking the recording of several of the articles for the accompanying audio CDs. The beautiful picture by Joaquín Sorolla which adorns the cover, *Jardín de la Casa Sorolla*, is reproduced by kind permission of Consuelo Luca de Tena, Director of the Museo Sorolla, Madrid, and Blanca Pons-Sorolla.

Raymond Calcraft
Elizabeth Matthews

Exeter
March 2016

List of Photographs

Front cover

Joaquín Rodrigo in the gardens of the Palace of Aranjuez 1989

Frontispiece

Joaquín Rodrigo in the 1960s

Preface

Joaquín Rodrigo was active as a writer from the late 1920s until some ten years before his death in 1999. The subjects he covered included the history of music, major composers and their works, outstanding musicians of his time, the arts in general, and his own life and music. Several articles were written during his thirty years as Professor of Music at the University of Madrid, but he had also worked previously, and for many years, as a concert reviewer and music correspondent, initially in Valencia, then for *Le monde musical* at the Salzburg Festival, and, after his return to Spain in 1939, for three newspapers in Madrid. Several scripts from his radio talks have also survived, together with addresses which he gave to academies and other institutions.

Almost the whole of this literary output is kept at the Victoria and Joaquín Rodrigo Foundation offices in Madrid, although a formal cataloguing of all Rodrigo's writings and interviews has still to be completed, in contrast to his music, all of which has now been published. An initial selection of the writings, in the original Spanish, appeared in 1999 under the title *Escritos de Joaquín Rodrigo*, edited by Antonio Iglesias. This only included a limited number of pieces, however, and does not do full justice to the range and variety of Rodrigo's skills as a writer.

The present volume is divided into two halves, the first dedicated to studies of major composers and their music, in chronological order, the second to the works and music of Rodrigo himself, again in order of dates of composition, with the exception of the first three and final articles. His extensive writings on other topics, the artists he knew and admired, his concert reviews and the numerous interviews he gave, will be included in a subsequent volume.

The articles have been translated directly and almost always without alteration from Rodrigo's original Spanish, although occasionally some minor editing has been found to be necessary. Several are quite long, though the majority are comparatively succinct, and a few, especially from the composer's later years, are very short, although they always contain details of interest. The date of each article or composition has been included wherever possible and there are three Appendices, *Personalia, Glossary* and *Publishers of Joaquín Rodrigo's Music*. The first gives brief details and dates for the less well-known composers and artists mentioned in the text; the second provides the basic meanings of several Spanish terms.

Foreword

Raymond Calcraft and Elizabeth Matthews are to be congratulated on the devoted service they have given to Rodrigo. These elegant and convincing translations cover the range of his thoughts on composition and composers, from Bach to Bruckner, delightful encounters with composers of his own time, Dukas and Falla, personal friends such as Segovia, and his own thoughts on composition and religion.

From reading his thoughts about his own compositions, I feel slightly more justified for some of the decisions we had to make when interpreting the composer's intentions. From playing his music, I believe I understand Rodrigo the composer; now I feel I know Rodrigo the man.

Sir Neville Marriner CBE

Joaquín Rodrigo the Writer

Raymond Calcraft

Joaquín Rodrigo lost his sight at the age of three, yet he became the leading Spanish composer of the second half of the 20th century, enjoying world-wide fame. His works include one of the best-loved of all pieces of classical music, the *Concierto de Aranjuez* for guitar and orchestra, but during the seventy-five years of his creative life he completed some one hundred and seventy compositions, written on his small Braille typewriter and painstakingly transcribed to a copyist. The works include eleven Concertos for a variety of instruments, a lyric opera, a ballet, music for the theatre and the cinema, several symphonic poems, a large quantity of instrumental music, in particular for solo piano and solo guitar, and sixty songs. Born on St Cecilia's Day in 1901 in the historic town of Sagunto, Valencia, Rodrigo's first composition dates from 1922. His last music was written in 1987, and he died in Madrid in July 1999.

During his life Rodrigo maintained an intense interest in many subjects, not only music. A friend of many years, Rafael Ibáñez, first engaged as a companion to the young Joaquín by Rodrigo's father, read many important works of literature to him, as well as history and philosophy, inculcating in Rodrigo a lasting love of knowledge. Rafael's work was initially supplemented and later succeeded, for the last seventy years of his life, by the person whom the composer himself called 'his eyes': his wife, Victoria Kamhi.

A reading of the *Catálogo completo* of Joaquín Rodrigo's music confirms the truth of his assertion that he considered himself to be above all a 'Spanish' composer, who gave idiomatic titles to all his works in his own language. In this he resembles composers of his time such as Debussy and Ravel, or the early Stravinsky, as well as his obvious predecessors in Spain, Albéniz, Granados and Falla. And whereas in the 1920s, when Rodrigo arrived in Paris to study with Paul Dukas, contemporaries such as Hindemith were embarking on a 'neoclassical' period, Rodrigo by contrast would proclaim his adherence to '*neocasticismo*' – a love of the culture of one's own country.

Joaquín Rodrigo was devoted to Spain, its culture, history, and literature. He never lost his affection for his native province of Valencia, but increasingly identified himself with Castile, whose capital, Madrid, was his home for the last sixty years of his life. Other regions of Spain, however, notably Andalusia, Catalonia and Galicia, were also sources of inspiration for him, in particular through the literature of their major writers. It is therefore not surprising that not a single title of a work by Rodrigo is known by its English equivalent. Manuel de Falla's three masterpieces with Andalusian settings – *El amor brujo, Noches en los jardines de España,* and *El sombrero de tres picos* – are all familiar from their English equivalents, but the titles of Rodrigo's works, even the most famous, are never translated. Thus *Concierto de Aranjuez* or *Fantasía para un gentilhombre,* with its delightful ambiguity, have to be understood and appreciated within an essentially Spanish context. *La traviata, La mer* and *Le tombeau de Couperin* are all works famously titled in their original languages, without the need for translation, and the same consideration has, perforce, to be extended to Joaquín Rodrigo's numerous compositions. The English-speaking listener, or reader, perhaps initially taken aback by titles such as *Ecos de Sefarad, El vendedor de chanquetes,* or *Sones en la Giralda,* will find that patiently discovering the meaning of them can add to the pleasure of understanding and enjoying the compositions to which they refer.

A love of literature seems to have been innate in Rodrigo, though it was doubtless developed by friends and relatives, who read to him constantly during his childhood and youth. Poetry, in particular, seems to have been a special interest and pleasure, and it is significant that in later life, when asked about his music, he indicated the songs as one of the most important areas of his work. From the earliest setting, in 1925, of a poem by the 15th-century dramatist Gil Vicente, to his last songs, in 1987, to words by his contemporary, Fina de Calderón, Rodrigo approached his chosen poets with unfailing understanding and imagination. An early masterpiece from 1934, *Cántico de la esposa,* to a text by St John of the Cross, was followed by a succession of compositions to words by writers of the stature of Miguel de Cervantes, Lope de Vega, and Rosalía de Castro, and the composer's contemporaries Miguel de Unamuno, Antonio Machado and Juan Ramón Jiménez. He also memorably set to music words from the Dead Sea Scrolls and the Bible, together with St Francis of Assisi's *Cantico delle creature*.

Joaquín Rodrigo was the last of a line of notable Spanish composers of the late 19th and 20th centuries, whose achievements during the remarkable flowering of the arts in Spain that took place following the military defeat of 1898 were comparable to those of the outstanding writers and artists of the time. A succession of fine novelists and poets, from Benito Pérez Galdós and Miguel de Unamuno to Federico García Lorca and Jorge Guillén, was paralleled in painting by Joaquín Sorolla, Pablo Picasso and Salvador Dalí, and in music by Isaac Albéniz, Enrique Granados and Manuel de Falla. And it is all the more remarkable that such a cultural phenomenon should have taken place in a Spain deprived of the last vestiges of a once great empire, and beset by the gravest political and social problems. The contrast with Spain's other 'Golden Age', where manifest achievement in all the arts took place within the context of world-wide imperial power and prestige, could not have been greater.

The 20th century was an era of extraordinary political change in Spain. Within Rodrigo's lifetime the country went from monarchy to dictatorship to republic, then through civil war to a second dictatorship, and finally to democracy and constitutional monarchy. As an ardent patriot, Rodrigo was never indifferent to any of these changes, but his stance towards his country and the events occurring within it, especially during the latter decades of the century, was resolutely apolitical. Virtually exiled in Germany and France during the Civil War, the Rodrigos returned to Spain in 1939 just before the start of the Second World War, his own country being then perhaps the only safe place for a blind man with a Jewish wife. Having established himself in Madrid, the composer became active in several public roles, including work for Radio Nacional, ONCE (the Spanish National Organisation for the Blind), and the University of Madrid, as the 'Manuel de Falla' Professor of Music. In his further role as music critic and correspondent for three newspapers in Madrid, Rodrigo was frequently critical of aspects of the arts and their organisation in Spain, but there is no indication in his articles of either overt support for, or direct criticism of, the government of the day. The many awards which Rodrigo received during his lifetime, under successive governments and from institutions both in his own country and abroad – from the *Légion d'Honneur* to the *Príncipe de Asturias* prize – reflected only the universal esteem and affection in which the composer and his music were held.

———

A young Spanish composer embarking on his career in the 1920s might perhaps have been expected to follow the example of his immediate Spanish predecessors in musical language and style. But even as a student in Valencia, Rodrigo's horizons were extending far beyond his own country, and he soon determined to follow the example of Albéniz, Falla and Turina by moving to Paris, then the principal artistic centre of Europe. Studying with Paul Dukas, meeting Falla, Honegger and Ravel, attending premières of the newest works by Stravinsky, all gave Rodrigo the necessary stimulus for both his own composing career and a broader education in music. In addition to his other gifts, and no doubt also due to his blindness, Rodrigo possessed an astonishingly retentive memory, so that, for example, almost everything heard and learnt in the five years he studied with Dukas was absorbed and put to creative use. It was in those classes, Rodrigo would recall, that the works of major composers were studied, analysed and discussed, alongside Dukas's critical assessment of the compositions which members of the class brought to him for comment and advice.

With this formative background, it is perhaps not surprising that Joaquín Rodrigo's first public lecture, at the Sorbonne in 1936, should have been on the subject of the 16th-century Spanish *vihuelistas* ('you know how much I love this music', he declared to his friend, Regino Sainz de la Maza). He would go on to write extensively, and for many decades, on every aspect of the music of Spain, from mediaeval Sephardic songs to the *zarzuelas* of Federico Moreno Torroba. But Paris, and Dukas, had made the entire history of European classical music a source of continual enlightenment and pleasure to Rodrigo. His writings, as a result, give as equal an importance to Mozart or Beethoven as to Antonio de Cabezón or Manuel de Falla, or to his own music and beliefs. 'I have tried to be faithful to a tradition', Rodrigo once remarked to me, but an initial assumption that this reference was exclusively to the culture of his own country is not necessarily correct, as his writings on the general history of music and its major composers suggest.

The interest shown by Rodrigo towards the music of composers other than those of his native Spain, from Monteverdi to contemporaries such as Stravinsky and Dallapiccola, is remarkable. Articles on Bach or Brahms could be expected, perhaps, but as early as 1950 he was also writing with both critical acumen and sympathy about Bruckner, for example, when that composer's reputation was nowhere near as high as it is today. Rodrigo's admiration for Verdi, which dated from his first experience of attending a performance of *Rigoletto* as a young man, is clear in several articles, and a particular aspect of Puccini's operas is likewise dealt with in an original way. It is clear that early exposure to the most avant-garde works in Paris encouraged Rodrigo to remain open to every new experience in music, whether it was attending the premières of Ravel's *Boléro* or Stravinsky's *Symphony of Psalms*, expressing admiration for a favourite work (Schoenberg's *Pierrot Lunaire*), naming Hindemith as perhaps the greatest composer of the 20th century, or learning about contemporary musicians in Chile.

The styles of writing deployed by Joaquín Rodrigo in these articles are as varied as the subjects they cover. Several pieces on Beethoven, for example, are essentially biographical and also include many surprising details concerning his life. Mozart's career is treated in a similar way, but in another article on him we find a short but illuminating assessment of the nature of his unique genius. Monteverdi's importance in the history of music is covered in some detail, while the same composer's background is the subject of a highly amusing history lesson delivered to an imaginary 'Amaryllis'.

Discussing and analysing his own music encouraged Rodrigo to write in similarly diverse ways. Some of the works are dealt with almost entirely through technical musical analysis, the inspiration behind others is suggested or made clear, and yet more are related directly to the history, the places, and even the artists who were their sources of inspiration. The composer clearly took as great a delight in speaking and writing his native language as he did in creating music inspired by Spain and its culture.

——

In the film *Shadows and Light: Joaquín Rodrigo at 90*, Cecilia Rodrigo asks her father why, having been so talkative in earlier years, he now seemed content to remain quite silent. He replies that it is more important for him now to 'meditar, reflexionar, pensar, observar, contemplar...', the rhythm of the synonyms falling away into silence, as though on an interrupted cadence. And when she asks him what he would still like to write, or to have written, he replies '¡Ah! ¡Un bello poema!'

Rodrigo was being too modest. As this selection of his writings shows, the composer frequently expressed himself memorably, and indeed poetically, about both his own music and that of others. In this he was exhibiting another facet of his remarkable creativity. Not only did he write about his art with insight, humour and eloquence; he also composed some of the most lyrically beautiful music of the 20th century.

Composers and their Music

Composers and their Music

Antonio de Cabezón, Organist to Philip II

This is not the first time that I have stated my belief, which grows stronger by the day, in the existence of a musical policy in the House of Austria. This policy, and I have no hesitation in calling it so, has already begun to be studied in France and Germany, and a precise evaluation of it would be one of the surest ways by which to enter the intricate labyrinth woven by the magic of polyphony.

It was a natural consequence that the political and military hegemony of the House of Austria during the 16th century should have also extended to music, given the passion felt for this art by those princes who had in fact received a very comprehensive musical education. This policy begins with the Emperor Maximilian, and reaches its apogee with Charles V and the princesses, later queens, who were his sisters.

Charles V will be the heir to the powerful Duchy of Burgundy, which reached as far as Flanders, and it is precisely in the borderland between these two regions where, from the time of Charles the Bold, and even before him, the remarkable Burgundian School starts to develop.

By a strange coincidence, in which perhaps unknown laws lie hidden which are not very far from the essence of music itself, the most prolific branch of western polyphony was to establish itself in the most sensitive place in Europe, where the fiercest battles of its history took place, which would change and alter its destiny. Here were born Dufay, Ockeghem, Josquin des Prés, Willaert, Orlando de Lassus and a host of illustrious disciples whose influence, via Venice, was made manifest in the magnificence of Roman polyphony, which was itself to inspire Spanish composers. However, it is in Spain where the Flemish and Burgundian currents from the North would converge with Italian lutenists, or more correctly, the Neapolitan School, which came from across the Mediterranean due to the expansion of Aragon into Italy. These two currents will criss-cross and fuse. Spain, led by the Catholic Monarchs (Ferdinand and Isabella) standing proudly on the threshold of the 16th century, is able to moderate these influences. They, in turn, and because of Spain's particular genius, develop into a magnificent school which subsequently becomes the golden age of our music – something we Spaniards still know little about.

To clarify, organise and compare these complex matters with critical rigour would be a formidable task, but one that would undoubtedly shed light on many aspects of our music, and especially in the case that is of interest to us here: the glorious maturity of that genius, Cabezón. And, particularly, on the still obscure origins of his education during the years from his birth, in 1510, until 1528, the year when, coming from Palencia, he enters the service of the Emperor.

This is the first information that we have of Antonio de Cabezón, the musician. Up to this point we know that he was born in a poor area of Castrogeriz and that he was blind from birth. He came from Palencia by recommendation of the Bishop of that diocese, where he must have studied both organ music and organ playing itself.

We must remember the important fact that Cabezón entered service in the Chapel of the Emperor at the age of eighteen. This indicates that not only was Cabezón perfectly able to carry out the duties of organist to the Court, but also – and this is of greater interest – that there was in existence a Spanish organ school which, even if it was not indigenous (the notion of the isolation of Spanish musicians is scarcely credible), already had sufficient standing and educative capacity to produce a musician who, youth notwithstanding, was to interact with the representatives of the powerful school of Hochheimer.

For the remainder of his life, thirty-six years, Cabezón remained at Court. He married there, 'for love, which is a great miracle', as Zapata would wittily say, and there he experienced the greatest pleasures, praise, triumphs and glory that any artist could dream of. He was assigned an annual income of 180,000 maravedís – an extraordinary amount, considering that Fuenllana, for example, who was Queen Isabel de Valois's musician, only received 53,000.

A permanent member of the household of the future king, Philip II, Cabezón would accompany him on his journey to Flanders, England, etc., in the role of principal organist and royal musician. This is the second detail in Cabezón's life that we should remember. He was fifty-three years old at the time, his genius fully apparent. For this first and only time, he left Spain to play in Italy and in Flanders, the cradle of Western music (a very unusual event among Spanish musicians in that period) and he would also be heard in the Tudor court, one of the most musical in Europe.

The impression that Philip II's organist created in those musical spheres was profound – they listened to him in astonishment. We need to seek the reasons for that response, for in it we will find the essence of the art of Cabezón. He undoubtedly demonstrated a formidable technique, but this would not have been all. Remarkable technique and extraordinary virtuosity were heard quite frequently in European courts. What was obvious to everyone in Cabezón was nothing less than an entire musical conception of a race, its aesthetic, its artistic position and its state of mind. For the first time in Europe the voice of Spanish mysticism was heard – uniquely privileged to resonate first in music, and some years later in poetry.

These journeys only confirm and increase the fame of Philip II's organist, the unrivalled, undisputed master of an illustrious constellation of organists. Cabezón was respected and venerated, and his death, which occurred in Madrid in 1566, was lamented by the King and Court as one would lament the loss of 'an inestimable jewel, an extraordinary talent'.

Cabezón's greatness should not surprise us. In the 15th and 16th centuries, and even earlier, from the time of Landino (the blind organist crowned with laurels in the presence of Petrarch in Florence), Cabezón was the musician par excellence, friend and master of kings and emperors, an idol of Christendom. His portative organ contained the voices of a thousand madrigal singers, and he set out before his astonished listeners the iridescence of its rich array of sounds, like a multi-coloured fan, sounds that were strangely similar to the human voice, together with trombones, flutes, trumpets and clarinets.

His daring fingers, moreover, swift and tireless, revealed an unknown world of sound, unexplored and disconcerting, which produced in the almost virgin ears of that time an ineffable and infinite ecstasy. What was actually taking place was the formation of a new art, the music of the Western world. This music was driven by two forces which were combined with one another. On the one hand, the popular songs and dances, the ballads, the music of the Court, spread throughout Europe by talkative ladies with their vihuelas, wandering musicians with portable organs strung round their necks, and elegant troubadours with their viols. On the other, the immense influence of Gregorian chant, established and taught by the monks of Cluny, and whose great flowering ends with the Cistercians. Thus Gregorian chant will be the inspiration for Cabezón's work, and chorales and variations will be the forms that contain his creative energy, into which he pours his genius. For this reason venerable Pedrell makes a very good point when, with all the enthusiasm of the discoverer of Cabezón, he calls him 'the Spanish Bach'. We could find many similarities in the work of the two composers, but their concept of music is diametrically opposed. The desire for the universal, for universal essence to be instilled into music, is externalised in the work of Cabezón by means of contemplation and ecstasy. In Bach these will be replaced by a Protestant exegesis, which inevitably has to have recourse to musical symbolism in sound, achieving in many works the impression of an illuminated manuscript.

Gregorian chant is the very expression of organic, natural, music, born in the depths of the pipes and stops of the organ. It is a child of ancient harmonic progressions yet is destined to bring about enormous developments. In Cabezón's hands is takes on its definitive form. For example: the versicles for the Service of Vespers; the *Magnificat*s that are the sublime culmination of his work; the wonderful *Variations on the 'Canto del Caballero'*. As an organist he had the best and the most complete instrument of the day, and could enjoy a wide range of forms that the madrigalists, being limited to the motet, lacked. Cabezón became the master of the art of playing *fantasías*, in the eloquent Spanish *tiento* form which, together with the *ricercar*, and ancient hunting tunes, were to bring us to the creation of the fugue. He approaches the variation (which had been developing from the time of Landino and before) in a more decorative way in his *Gallarda milanesa*. He eventually realised that everything had to have an instrumental character, to have its own style. This style, enlivened by the individuality of the popular songs that he used to listen to as a child in the vastness of Castile, would set him apart from the other organists of his day.

But, notwithstanding the commentary already made, what strange force is it that breathes through this music and gives it its profound life? Something that the cleverest and most penetrating analyses cannot fathom, and that Pedrell pointed to so accurately when he said, 'inspiration has passed over these pages'. The voice of Spanish mysticism, as I said at the beginning.

Cabezón is a brother to Fray Luis de León. He inscribes on his deep and massive musical staves in the same way that Fray Luis engraves his poetry. His work expresses the same noble serenity, the same heavenly vision. And thus 'the air becomes serene, clothed in beauty and light uncommon' when, slowly, calmly, transfigured by grace, the harmonies descend from the organ of Antonio de Cabezón, like those of Salinas, 'guided with wisdom by his hand'.

c 1940

On the 300th Anniversary of the Death of Claudio Monteverdi

It would be wrong to think that music in the 16th century was only used for religious expression. The 16th century, which we should consider as the last century of mediaeval music, expressed a great deal in secular forms, and it is this aspect which we must take as the starting point if we wish to understand Monteverdi, and not be surprised at his emergence into the world of music.

THE MADRIGAL

Secular music develops in four areas, in four different ways, with four cardinal points within a world of sound, placed at the service of a single ideal: to entertain, to amuse, to delight. Two of these forms, destined for such exalted heights, pertain to instrumental music. There was music for dancing and instrumental music its own right. This latter was 'invented' – to use their own delightful expression – by the most celebrated musicians on earth, the organists, the vihuelists, the lutenists and the players of the clavichord. A third was a combination of forms, the accompanied song. Voice and instrument would produce startling pieces, in which the cultured and the popular would be mixed in unusual ways. Finally, the fourth type used as its vehicle the same vocal forms as were used in the Church, the same technical procedures as that music, and which threatened to corrupt it. It was the madrigal.

All these new forms in which secular music presented itself throughout the 16th century were fully evolved; they were the heritage of the 15th and even the 14th century. They will become, in terms of pure musical contribution, the stimulus for opera, and will be assimilated in varying degrees into it. Opera is, in fact, the first result of the desire for synthesis, or the ideal, even, which leads to the discovery and achievements of sung theatre. But for the purposes of this survey, and as a clear and direct way forward, only the last two types matter: the songs, ballads and verses that were sung to the accompaniment of vihuela or lute, and the beautiful madrigal, the solo voices of which resonated beneath the decorated ceilings of Italian Renaissance palaces.

All kinds of licence and liberties, prohibited in religious polyphony because of the very nature and purpose of that music – and not, as has been said, for capricious reasons – were permitted in the madrigal, a composition which differed in outward terms from the motet (the form used in church music) by the use of a secular text or theme, sonnets, madrigals, dirges, songs, or – in Spain – folksongs and carols. Here it was possible to give free rein to descriptiveness, as old as music itself, to onomatopoeia, always an outlet for humour in music, and to the desire to obtain from sound a level of expressiveness through which to awaken strong feelings, sometimes purely sensorial (unusual combinations of chords, chromatic sequences, etc.), sometimes emotional. Musicians also wanted to interpret the joys and sorrows of human life, and they wished to write about love, war, celebration; to express hatred; to sing of the sweetness of love, or the bitter pleasure of jealousy.

In order to achieve all this, styles change. Counterpoint, or lineal composition, is too restrictive, and it is not sufficiently intimate. Influenced by players and, above all, guided by instinct and necessity, musicians gradually modify their compositions, which become more simple (in fact, more affected). Harmony, sonority and musical impact prevail over the independent line or melody. Everything is done to interpret the poetic text in the best and most faithful way, searching for effect and expression. A kind of race begins, which becomes increasingly wild, where the musicians try to achieve all these, and boldness, creativity and innovation take over. The years from 1550 to 1600 recall the period between 1900 and 1940. Cipriano de Rore is typical of this time and Prince Carlo Gesualdo outdoes it with his extravagance. Music loses in purity and control what it gains in grace and expressiveness. They say that musicians thought more in terms of 'painting' feelings, than in music. A new age is beginning.

THE PRECURSERS

Parallel to this restless investigation by the madrigalists into the nature and possibilities of sound, there developed a logical progression among eminent humanists, poets and artists, the intellectuals of the time. As a consequence of Renaissance ideas, they wanted to achieve a similar renaissance in music, and recreate nothing less than the music of ancient Greece. Nowadays we are starting to see more clearly what this music was like, even though we cannot hear it. But in the 16th century there were no other hypotheses.

In salons and discussion groups the ghost of Greek music rises up, and those lovers of music (today we would call them musical snobs) give their opinions in the most serious manner, even to the point of decreeing what the music composed for the tragedies of Sophocles and Euripides was like, how it sounded, what it aimed to achieve, and what effects it created. Music had to be at the service of words so as to bring out their meaning, to elevate and increase their emotive power; but not in the manner of the most extravagant and audacious madrigalists who were still, in spite of everything, in thrall to the inclusiveness of counterpoint. It had to be individualised music, a kind of lyrical, expressive 'declaiming'.

By about 1580, the famous Florentine 'Camerata', whose members used to meet in the palace of Count Giovanni de' Bardi, began to be influential. They developed with particular vehemence the theories of a group of artists who were tired of the incredible cathedrals of sound constructed by Palestrina, but who would go into ecstasies over an unexpected chord, whispered by a theorbo, or faint at the rippling portamenti from the heavenly voice of a castrato. And out of these lucubrations, fantasies and inspirations, the opera was conceived. On 6th October 1600, a wonderful musico-literary construct called *Euridice*, created by the singer and organist Jacopo Peri and the poet Ottavio Rinuccini, was put on during the celebrations for the marriage of Henry IV, King of France, with Maria de' Medici. Opera was born. The great professional musicians, who looked with scorn and ridicule at the enthusiasts who had invented it ('inventors' is the right name for Jacopo Peri, Giulio Caccini and Emilio Cavalieri), could not imagine the role reserved for them in the history of music.

II

If it were not for the terrible convulsions that are ravaging Europe at the moment, this date, 29th November 1943, which marks the third centenary of the death in Venice of Claudio Monteverdi, would be celebrated in Italy, and in every other country, with festivals, studies and anniversary conferences, denoting the loss of one of the greatest geniuses of music – the musician who laid the foundations of the most wonderful edifice of sound: opera.

For me, and for many others, Monteverdi is the epicentre of the greatest seismic shift in the history of music. It was a veritable earthquake, which did not so much shake the foundations of our art, as destroy them. It brought to an end an entire age, at the very moment when music had achieved a level of such perfection, richness and universality – this is the expression which best and most exactly describes the style of that epoch – that it seemed that those forms of writing were unassailable, untouchable. Clearly, I am referring to what is understood as the age of polyphony, at its height from Dufay (c 1397 – 1474) to Palestrina (c 1525 – 1594).

In broad terms, the music of the 16th century had one essential form, counterpoint, and it used the human voice as its instrument. But this particular human voice, which ninety per cent of the time belonged to the Church, avoided individuality. Inspired by the Catholic ideal, it submerged its individuality in the anonymity of horizontality, that is to say, the various vocal lines which operated independently, even to the point where they were written on separate sheets of paper. It was deemed a technical weakness to write one voice part together with another. This is what we do today, in what is called a musical score, without which it would be impossible to compose. But the very act of subjecting the human voice to the most impersonal of styles and compositions, of trying to express the universal by means of man's most personal attribute, his voice (which has to use language), led to the principal mistake, the obvious contradiction – a weakness which very soon was bound to be disastrous. Musicians' contempt for everything except the music became so complete that in a composition for four voices or more, which formed such wonderful, homogeneous music that its like has never been achieved since, not only did they not care if the text could not be understood, or that some poetry would begin and then some more would enter half way through (unavoidable in practice), but they would also insert various different texts, and in different languages. Thus, while the tenor sang the Credo from the Mass, the bass, in similar, often identical, music, would sing a popular love song, to which the soprano would respond with a jolly little ditty which was often quite inappropriate.

The composer of polyphony did not need inspiration in the same way as we understand this magical word, and especially not in the way that the Romantics understood it. Moreover, our way of feeling and composing simply would not have been understood by him. All he needed was a 'cantus firmus' – that is to say, a melodic line provided by a Gregorian melody, a religious hymn, or a popular song. Around this line, ideally above it and below it, others were constructed so that, sustained by this veritable spinal column, he expressed the inexpressible, the ineffable, the eternal. Today, listening to it, it seems to us divine. For the composer of those times there was nothing but the pure, formal beauty of the musical line, in accordance with the rules of harmony, which were few – a small group of sonorous intervals, and combinations of serene sounds. It was a music whose profusion of intertwined and superimposed notes seemed to make it live in abstract space.

It is easy to understand that, musically speaking, the 16th century is anachronistic: it existed by and for the Church. Eighty per cent of that music was sung in Latin. The profane breezes that stirred the trees of Parnassus at the end of the 15th century hardly affected it. It took no notice of the Renaissance. In the actual composition of music, it was ignorant of the currents of Humanism, even though it praised them. It was scarcely interested at all in the new theories concerning sound, or the early ventures into physics.

The archetypal composer of polyphony is Palestrina. All facets of music seem to come together in two composers: in Palestrina, the master from Rome, for his emblematic, perfect music, and his extraordinary technique; and in Orlando de Lassus, the Flemish master, for his limitless universality. These two sum up that age which, while composing perfect circles of sound in which they believed firmly and securely, they themselves were undermining. They did not realise that those circles rested on assumptions that were very serious for contemporary intellectuals. There was no convergence with the aesthetic currents of the time; they openly despised and ignored the instrumental music heard in the great houses, which was soon to take over and create a new form of musical expression, claiming for itself the authority that comes from innovation. At the same time that

Palestrina was publishing his celebrated *Missa Papae Marcelli* (c 1562), the masterpiece of the Counter Reformation, Monteverdi, who would bring an end to polyphony, was born in Cremona. Only a composer nurtured by polyphony, brought up on it, educated to respect the old style and eschew the theorisers, could first of all adopt its rules and later be able to change them into others as profound, if not as eternal.

1943

Letters to Amaryllis

Listening to Italian Renaissance Composers

It is wrong of you, my dear Amaryllis, to speak so amusingly of your horror of musical history. When one lives in the world of ambition and talent, with the privileges of temperament and vocal ability, it is necessary to support them with at least a minimum of the facts which only history can provide. Yes, I know, you always tell me that history is boring, but I am also ambitious and have decided, if not to amuse you, at least to guide you by giving you some elementary lessons in the history of music – that music which you now sing not at all badly, it is true, in spite of being unforgivably ignorant of history!

You must know, dear Amaryllis, that in the 15th and 16th centuries music was made by 'cantors' – no, don't flatter yourself yet, 'cantors' (I haven't written 'singers' – they would come later) were almost always priests or courtiers who gathered together to sing in two, four or eight parts. Princes and aristocrats maintained impressive groups of performers which they called 'capelle' (which is where the phrase to 'sing *a capella*' comes from), meaning to sing together without instrumental accompaniment, even though the 'capellae' of that period did have instruments. Some aristocrats also took part in them – like King Louis XII of France, or Prince Juan, the first-born son of the Catholic Monarchs – and travelled with them, as Queen Isabella always did, even when at war. Those musical groups, amongst which were the very famous ones of the emperor Charles V, the kings of France, and the Sistine Chapel, performed both sacred and secular music. The only thing that mattered to these musicians – this will seem a cliché to you, although it isn't – was music for music's sake, expression in sound in and of itself, that is, the art of combining sounds in time. What was sung, the *words*, mattered very little, in spite of the poets' texts which were set, and who cared whether they were understood or not? What a joy, don't you think? How happy all you Amaryllises would be if we didn't annoy you with our endless 'can't understand a word you sing'!

I have already told you that what mattered was music for music's sake: counterpoint, combinations, imitations of one voice by another, the constant sequences, fugues, etc., everything we understand by the word 'canon'. Not much of what was sung was understood, not because it wasn't pronounced, but because of the nature of those compositions, which required the singers, when they sang, for example, 'Chloris was combing her hair in the sun with her alabaster hand, with a golden comb', to do the following: when the tenor was singing 'alabaster hand', the soprano was singing 'golden comb', and the bass joined in this nonsense exclaiming 'Chloris her hair'! And not just this. Many works were sung in Italian, French and Spanish at the same time, or words were mixed up one after the other in different languages, even dialects. The degradation of music went even further in this blessed period of musical history. Masses were sung in which one voice would intone, with its particular text, a popular or well-known song – which might be martial or amorous. So the tenor, for example, would utter his amorous complaint, grieving for some Amaryllis or other (they had them then too), while the other voices replied 'Kyrie eleison'!

However, outside this music, noblest of all, purest of the pure, another way of singing was developing, the vocal solo. The first collections of this music, part vocal, part instrumental, appeared in the first years of the 16th century in Italy, followed quickly by France and Spain. The first of these books, in fact, was published in Valencia in 1535–36, and the composer was the noble Valencian, Luis de Milán, a fine gentleman, an aristocratic courtier, and both a great musician and a vain Don Juan, who modestly gave himself the titles of 'Successor to Orpheus' and 'Ladies' grief'. This new music lived almost entirely from borrowings. It sang popular refrains or happily lifted the most melodic parts from great choral works. In this way, the solo voice, accompanied by the lute or vihuela in simple form, allowed what was being sung – and here is the danger for you singers! – to be clearly heard.

You can't imagine, Amaryllis, the success which this trick, like all tricks, had. These musicians, extraordinarily skilled instrumentalists – geniuses, in fact – and excellent singers, were the spoilt children of the courts, and without anyone realising it, they were undermining the high, proud walls behind which the imprisoned Palestrinas, Lassuses, Victorias and Legrenzis were raising their sonorous spires to the heavens, or creating madrigals full of audacious sounds.

And you will see what happened, which will fill you with both delight and fear at the same time. But I see that reading this is beginning to tire you, so let us leave it for another letter, if you promise me that you will read it!

––––

In spite of your lively protests at my having called you totally ignorant of the history of music, your reply, which proves that you have read my letter from beginning to end, inspires me to continue with these brief history lessons, a kind of trivial pursuit for a musicologist! Before ending this first chapter, then, I want you to see, dear Amaryllis – in case others wiser than you, although less artistic, should read me – that in my desire to make these lessons more pleasant for you, I have disguised certain facts and exaggerated others.

So, for example, we have the contempt of composers for the texts which they set to music (I wouldn't want poets to become too enraged, if they thought that, and take reprisals against us composers!). Especially in the 16th century, and after the first third in particular, one can see an attention and a care to use music to underline the action or the lyricism of the chosen texts – our Tomás Luis de Victoria in his 'Passions', Prince Gesualdo in his daring madrigals, or the Burgundian musicians, masters of the madrigalesque song, without even mentioning the great Palestrina, or the huge figure of Orlando de Lassus, the most universal yet paradoxical composer of that age – all of them showed their interest in that kind of expression. But even so the words remained in the attic of their aesthetic intentions, like a poor relative. And now we go on to that cataclysm, and joy for you, which I spoke to you about before, and in which you are so interested.

The Renaissance brought amongst other things the knowledge of the Greek and Latin classics which the Middle Ages had either not known about or had forgotten. Hence its name. Their works were translated and even their tragedies and comedies were performed, in which music – especially in the former – took such an important part that words, music and dance formed a completely unified whole. But what could not be translated, as a result of having been largely lost, and through ignorance of the musical notation employed by the Greeks, was the music over which the actors declaimed their words. Note the word I have just used, 'declaimed'.

Renaissance artists were not daunted by so small a thing, and set off along the attractive path of conjecture, borne on the wings of their imaginations. And some enthusiasts for music, men of sensitivity and artistic spirit, who gathered at the famous meetings of Count Bardi in Florence (what idiocies must have been uttered in those meetings of such 'special' spirits!), after much shouting and discussion, much joking, and clever, ironic or ingenious phrases, agreed and declared that the most important musicians of the time, whose technique still astonishes us, were just annoying; that all those many-voiced madrigals, and the magnificent works of polyphony (polyphony is the art of writing for many voices in which each must be sufficient unto itself and have its own significance within a common domain) was music that was out of date. They maintained that so many voices together just gave one a headache, and that it had no interest any more, because it didn't excite anybody, it did not move them ('move' – another word which you, as a singer, should take note of). And they thought that music should be written like that of the Greeks, and since no-one knew what that was like, it should be invented. Down with Palestrina and that great constellation of composers of his time, unbearable old fogies who did not know how to express emotion, or how to 'move' the listener! They themselves *were* going to 'move'!

As I told you, those who spoke like this and were about to act were, compared to the masters whom they were attacking, enthusiasts, half poets, half musicians, 'singers', in fact, not 'cantors'. Like David against Goliath, they marched against the fortress of polyphony, carrying no weapons except a harp, a lyre or a lute – the latter being the preferred instrument – and those other arms which seemed so insignificant, but which were in fact frightening: the voice, and declamation. The art of singing had been born!

The advancing foot soldiers of that fierce musical war were the collections of madrigals for a single voice, which all those foolish composers wrote and, above all, sang. These collections of 'new music' (as the composers modestly called it) were written by Galileo, del Cavaliere, Jacomo Peri and by Caccini, the most gifted of them all: 'when Caccini sang, accompanying his madrigals to Amaryllis on the lute, his heavenly voice and purest diction made us shed copious tears, to the point where we thought we would dissolve!'

To move, to declaim, to sing – here, dear Amaryllis – is what those musicians achieved who rode into view between the 16th and 17th centuries. But a bulwark was needed, nevertheless, from which the final assault could be made upon counterpoint. And this was opera.

Based on what Greek tragedy might have been, those enthusiasts invented an artistic form in which things were acted and sung, or rather, declaimed – since the music had to serve the poetry, enhance it, take it further, augment the expressive power of the words. For this reason those musicians didn't just sing wonderfully but developed declamation and gesture, so that every inflexion of the voice was accompanied by a clear, distinct word, in the purest and clearest Italian, supported by a face whose expressions underlined perfectly the meaning of the text. In this way the voice was like a catapult which launched the words and the music as far as possible, with the deepest possible emotion.

The triumph of singers was overwhelming and complete – this was the joy that had been anticipated – but the terrible thing is that they swept away and destroyed the old masters. The proud citadels of counterpoint came tumbling down, and during the first quarter of the 17th century, even during Victoria's lifetime, the musical world turned its back on them – that music was now just in ruins. A real earthquake had shaken the foundations of music and those audacious spirits were right – a new kind of music had been born, the opera! I will tell you about that in my next letter.

THE OPERA

In 1600 what we could call the first opera was staged. In fact it was just an experiment. The work was *Euridice,* and its composer Jacopo Peri. The Florence 'Camerata' did things well (you will remember that the 'camerata' was a meeting in the palace of the nobleman Bardi, in which the greatest insults were hurled at the best music of the time). The work was chosen as part of the extraordinary festivities celebrating the occasion of the marriage of Henry IV of France and Maria de' Medici. It was a tremendous success, in spite of the fact that the work was no more than a sketch for an opera; even so, everyone cried 'A miracle, a miracle!', and it was seriously affirmed that classical tragedy had been reborn.

Nevertheless, this, with one or two other attempts, could not have overcome the older forms of musical expression in a way that would survive – this was an intellectual success only. What was necessary was a truly musical one, and this was *Orfeo*, by Claudio Monteverdi, of which you know a few outstanding excerpts.

Monteverdi had been born in 1567, that is, when the art of polyphony was at its height, when no-one thought of any other music but that. Monteverdi was educated in counterpoint and became very skilled at it, even though from his first works – various books of madrigals – he was drawn to the ideal of expressing and interpreting poetic texts. He is soon fascinated by the new theories concerning music, and even though he is not a member of the 'Camerata', he seeks out and reads their writings and pamphlets. He is the man the new music needs, because he is the genius which every new development requires in order to triumph.

The performance of *Orfeo* – in 1600, I think (I am on holiday and do not have my books with me) – was a revelation, and ecstatically received.

This was in fact the first opera, since with its decorations, its costumes and the scenery in which soloists, chorus, dancers and orchestra took part, there was continuous dramatic action. The orchestra, for example, was very numerous, very colourful and basic. Just imagine, you could see in it, or rather hear, zithers, lutes, harps, violins of various sizes – which were played sometimes on the shoulder, sometimes on the musician's knees – trumpets, flutes, small organs and cymbals

The choice of the myth of Orpheus was not a matter of chance. Monteverdi, like Gluck after him, who would deal with the same story one hundred and fifty years later, chose this myth because he felt an affinity for it. You know that a serpent wounds Euridice, the adored wife of Orpheus, who dies as she is gathering flowers to present to him; this is what he is told by the messenger in whose arms she has expired. Orpheus merely cries out 'Alas, woe is me!', but he immediately recovers himself. He knows the power of music, he knows that he has often calmed the most ferocious wild animals, and that storms and the whole of nature itself seem to become serene when he sings. He takes his lyre and descends to hell to rescue Euridice from it. He begs, implores, weeps, but above all 'sings', that is, declaims; every word gains greater and more original expression, because it is conveyed on the wings of music. For this reason above all it is vital that every comma, every interjection and every accent should be emphasised by deep sighs and silences, after which the music renews its power. The furies become calm, are moved, and give back to Orpheus his adored Euridice. The power of declamation in music!

But this event only takes place amongst the nobility. Several years have still to pass. Monteverdi leaves Ferrara and his prince, and goes to Venice. There the first opera house will be opened. The success is so great that soon several others are opened, and in a very few years the whole of Italy sees opera houses appear in every city. The passion which Italians feel for opera can only be compared with that which Americans feel for the cinema.

But – alas! – soon the ideal of the Florentines is lost; singers – singers, Amaryllis! – wanted to sing, not to move people or to serve the music, but to show off. And so we began to hear the trills, the chirping and the cackling which you quite rightly dislike so much. The Monteverdian ideal, which he himself renounced in his later years (he lived a very long life, and old people do go a bit soft), resulted in him taking refuge with Carissimi in the oratorio – a kind of sacred opera – or resorting to the instrumental field, about which I shan't write to you, as you don't play an instrument – an absolute and unpardonable sin, of which you will one day repent.

The Florentine school moves to France and the opera, in spite of Cesti and even Alessandro Scarlatti, remains moribund. The most eminent souls write ferocious diatribes against it, and singers, always the singers…!

Don't be upset though, Amaryllis. It wasn't all weeping and desolation. It's true that more operas sprang up than mushrooms, and more musical salesmen than true composers. But if the deepest musical expression died in Italy, the grace and seductive lines of the Neapolitan song were born, whose first genius was the elder Scarlatti.

The Bicentenary of Johann Sebastian Bach

To avoid going astray in the intricate, sonorous labyrinth of Bach's colossal output, we need to classify it, to divide it into groups. I am not sure, but, since everything has been written about Bach, I imagine that his serious biographers will have indicated what I would call the four directions of his work. And here I am not meaning to compare them with the famous three styles of Beethoven, which in reality are nothing more than the evolution of the one style, his own. Similarly, in Bach we find only the one style, his own, not specific, either, to his time, since in that period there were several styles. But it is certainly characteristic of his age, though not very obviously apparent, as I have written elsewhere. But his interests, together with the requirements of his time, allied to the notion that composers and their audiences then had of themselves as artists, led Bach to write music which could be classified into four significant chapters, as I have said.

The first, numerically, comprises the large quantity of music that came about purely for practical reasons – Bach wanted and needed to teach not only the organ, but also the piano and even the violin. It is a considerable number of works, which managed to disguise their didactic intent with attractive titles for charming music. This group of works was also responsible for the relative popularity that he enjoyed during his lifetime, and the reason why he was not totally forgotten in the fifty years following his death. We need to realise as we listen that this music was created for educational purposes, which explains a certain pleasure in setting up all kinds of musical challenges that at times irritate us, or spoil our enjoyment.

The second group comprises those works most familiar to the general public. Those that, in the main, fall into the category of music for the court, mostly written at the request of princes, or otherwise for purely practical or economic reasons. To this group belong the orchestral suites, the concertos and the pieces written for solo instrument, though there is a difference here between the latter pieces and the solo pieces in the first group. Even though the music of this group is the best known and the most frequently played, it is not by any means the most typical of Bach. On many occasions he had to go against his own taste and inclinations in order to write them.

Even so, from some of these pieces there develops the third group, where we find the heart of Bach. That is to say, it is music that takes Bach gradually but unequivocally towards abstraction and mathematical speculation about the nature of music. The purest demonstrations of this come in *The Musical Offering* and *The Art of Fugue*, respectively, together with various chorales.

Finally, we come to the most important group, to which Bach himself drew attention and in which we find the key to everything else: the religious music, which is the pure, essential Bach.

People have emphasised the Protestantism of Bach's music. Without wishing to deny that that is the case to a very great extent, I find that I am not able to make a judgement on this from personal knowledge. We know very well to what extent Bach was an orthodox Lutheran, but not far from that firmly held faith is the ideal of a Christianity that would bring to an end, on the cross, all the different interpretations of dogma – which was a constant vision for Bach.

A Mozart Anniversary

Wolfgang Amadeus Mozart was born one hundred and eighty-seven years ago today.

If Beethoven represents the end of Classicism and the beginning of a new era for musicians, an era which is still in existence now, then the brief life of Wolfgang Amadeus Mozart (27th January 1756 – 5th December 1791) encompasses the short time that Classicism itself lasted. Before him, in fact, the sonata and the symphony, which are the first expressions of Classicism, had no clear, specific structures, nor can they be defined in a strict and exact way. After Mozart, not even Haydn could bring anything new to the 18th century, in spite of his *Oxford Symphony* of 1789 or his *London Symphony* of 1791.

Mozart not only gives Classicism stability, he also brings together all the musical tendencies of his era. In a truly exceptional and unique way, in the whole history of music, he was able to assimilate his contemporaries' different national characteristics, whose variety of styles cannot be clearly appreciated today because of their distance in time. Having absorbed these various styles, he would then transform them into a homogeneous whole, by means of the most extraordinary developments. The resulting balance and synthesis are what we understand as 'Mozart's music'. This explains perfectly the indifference, almost, towards his work of all those many musicians who, in order to be moved, need powerful, thrilling arpeggios (Scarlatti); splendid, sonorous pauses (Handel); overwhelming rhythmic power (Bach); huge, emotive harmonies (Rameau); or even simple wit (Haydn). We find none of these musical extremes in Mozart because they have all been refined and absorbed.

On the basis of this, it has been possible for those who enjoy paradoxes to defend the thesis that the greatest composer of the 18th century was the least original. As far as I am concerned, Mozart has always been the most difficult of the 18th century masters, the least understood, in terms of his genius, and, for this reason, poorly appraised. Frequently we cannot understand Bach, but there is always something there that takes us by surprise and we intuit his greatness. Mozart never takes us by surprise, he is not to be 'intuited'; he has to be understood, and to 'understand', in terms of music, is the most difficult thing of all.

Everything about Mozart is marvellous. His infancy is like a fairy tale. On that night of the 27th January 1756, the carillon from the tower of the Italianate cathedral of Salzburg must have made the evocative cadences of 'Prinz Eugen, der edle Ritter'[1] sound more clear and crystalline than ever. Yes, indeed, Wolfgang was to be 'the noblest prince' in the most beautiful story in music.

Three years later, his father, a severe musician who came from the north of Germany, a grim man, little given to fantasies, was amazed, transported, by his little boy who was playing on the piano his first, accomplished flights of notes. A year later, at the age of four, Wolfgang composed his first work, a minuet, and began to play the spinet correctly. Two years later, Mozart went on the first of his tours. And so began the marvellous excursions, the visits to all the courts of Europe, both large and small. The child played, composed, improvised and enjoyed himself with all the gifts, the applause and the flattery. Kings and emperors invited him to their tables, the most beautiful princesses played with him on their laps, delighted by that most extraordinary of playthings. Wolfgang, offering his hand to the most beautiful, promised to marry her, since she was the one who had been able to dry his tears after he tripped and fell on the flagstones in the palace – it was Marie Antoinette. Months later it would be Paris which admired the prodigy and claimed glory for itself by publishing his first works, four Sonatas, in 1763.

Mozart travelled to London and met Johann Christian Bach, (one of the sons of the great Johann Sebastian), who was musician to the King. With this excellent guide, the young composer would make great strides. Christian, amazed, spent hours listening to the child improvise and set him numerous musical conundrums which the youngster solved without any difficulty. Soon afterwards Mozart would write his first opera, *La finta semplice,* commissioned by the Emperor of Austria in 1766, and the following year he was appointed director of concerts in the Archbishop's Palace in Salzburg. That same year he undertook his triumphant journey to Italy, where Pope Clement XIV made him a member of the Order of the Golden Spur.

Italy! Whoever says Italy explains half of Mozart. After all, isn't Mozart the greatest Italian composer of the 18th century? Italy's enthusiasm for this young man is difficult to describe. But soon the intrigues and jealousies appear; Wolfgang is no longer a child; a series of operas and diverse compositions do not achieve the acclaim due to them. Salzburg no longer recognises Mozart as its very own genius, and is indifferent to his departure in 1775.

Unable to find in the innumerable German courts a well-paid post or a place where he would be understood and appreciated, Mozart began his last journey to Paris in 1778. He was twenty-two years old, a young man whose fairy-tale infancy and adolescence had come to an end. To make his awakening all the more bitter, it all ended in a failed love affair with Aloysia Weber, an excellent singer, who later would take part in some of his opera premières, and who would become his sister-in-law.

Difficult times lay ahead for Mozart. His beloved mother died in Paris and, alone, unhappy and unsuccessful, he returned to Salzburg to further suffering at the hands of his volatile father, from whom he would finally separate by departing for Vienna in 1781. He was twenty-six years old and only had a scarce nine years of life remaining. But in those few years he wrote a series of absolute masterpieces that nobody will ever surpass. Although Emperor Joseph II received him and appointed him Director of Music, it was in fact a modest position and poorly paid. Although Haydn claimed he was the greatest composer of all, Mozart's life was hard and difficult. An independent musician at last, he certainly experienced the ups and downs of fate, freely able to express his genius but also worried about the future, with a wife and five children to support.

Weak and exhausted, with scarcely the strength to hold the pen with which he had written more than six hundred works in less than thirty years, Wolfgang wrote the *Requiem* in the certain knowledge that it would be his own.

And so it was. On 5th December 1791, alone, forgotten by everyone, Mozart died in Vienna, the Vienna that he had loved so much and did not want to leave, in spite of tempting offers from the King of Prussia, the only person who truly understood his worth. And while he was being buried in a pauper's grave, for there was nothing but debt at home, people in the Wieden Theatre were laughing, as they listened to the innocent slapstick of Papageno and Papagena.

1942

---

[1] 'Prince Eugene, the noble knight', a German folksong about the victory of Prince Eugene of Savoy in 1717 during the Austro-Turkish War of 1716–1718.

Something Unique to Mozart

Something that seems to me to be unique to Mozart, without going into detail about his musical activity, is the unusual similarity between the amazement that he caused amongst the first audiences who heard him, and the most recent audiences to hear him, those of today, two hundred years later. I think that there are no precedents for this, just as there have been no recurrences since. Those who watched and listened to the infant Mozart for the first time had a premonition that something unparalleled was about to occur. We certainly know the accuracy of that prophecy. And just as no genius was hailed with such enthusiasm from his very beginnings, neither has any other been followed with such devotion. From 1800 on, posterity has proclaimed and confirmed the genius of that child, in whom so many believed, and, for more than a century and a half, admiration for, and pleasure in, his music have remained unchanged. Classicism expired, the storms of Romanticism rolled by, the shimmering chalice of Impressionism opened out, Brutalism erupted, Burlesque sprang up, Intellectualism shone serene and bright, Expressionism was anguished about everything – 'What Does It All Mean?' And all these infinitely varied tendencies, modes and fashions turned the same smiling face towards Mozart. The only reason for this unique phenomenon lies in the fact that Mozart is the synthesis, the ultimate balance, the single point from which can be viewed the two great arcs of Western music, the one which takes us to the birth of Classical form, and the one which is perhaps leading us towards the beginnings of a new age.

A Dispatch from Vienna
on the 150th anniversary of the death of Mozart

The kind invitation from the German government, whom we can never thank enough, wings us to Vienna in a powerful four-engined Lufthansa plane. We are four Spaniards: Joaquín Turina, José Forns, Federico Sopeña and me. As a preparation for this unforgettable 'Mozart Week', which the German government has organised with almost scientific precision, this baptism by air is quite appropriate – it takes us there in gentle flight towards that other music which was, uniquely, like angels' wings.

Arrival in Vienna is always a deeply emotional pleasure. We feel the same dizziness that has overtaken us before, when we think of the composers who have lived in this city beside the Danube. It is a curious thing, this influence that some cities have on the development and nature of the arts. Just as it would be difficult to understand Spanish painting without Madrid, so it would be impossible to enter the dense forest of German music without knowing and understanding Vienna. But, let us set aside these serious thoughts and outline briefly what has happened during this unforgettable Mozart Week.

Let us see how those who control musical life in the Third Reich have organised what I like to call the three-part Mozart arrangement – that is to say, morning, noon and night! Over eight days, this means there are twenty-four concerts during the official Mozart Week alone, given that the Vienna City Council also puts on at the same time events dedicated to that musical genius who sums up the entire 18th century.

It was necessary to achieve two formidable objectives during this Week. First: to give a comprehensive vision of the harmonious breadth of Mozart's music – not an easy thing to do if we consider that Mozart wrote over six hundred works in thirty years. And it should not be forgotten that classical composers modestly combined within a small number of works several compositions whose length and importance would have taken several years for a composer of today. Second: to provide a model, an example, for the way to interpret this music, given that the Mozart Week takes place before the musical worlds of Europe and of Germany itself. So, this last objective is of great importance for us, as we are very interested to know the criteria used to interpret Mozart, one hundred and fifty years after his death.

Germany begins by concentrating a large part of its musical resources in Vienna. The foundation of this is the marvellous Vienna Philharmonic Orchestra, upon which has fallen an exhausting task. It is well known that the Vienna Philharmonic seems to have been born to play Mozart. A long succession of great conductors, which continues today, has transformed it into one of the finest and most flexible orchestras that I know. The lightness and speed of the string section sometimes sends shivers down your spine, and the woodwind this time seems to me to be softer and more unified than ever. And what can one say of the horns, whose accuracy and clarity of attack sounds like a piano being played. Sharing events with the Philharmonic is the Vienna Symphony Orchestra – younger, but of obvious reliability. In addition to these orchestras, and sometimes made up from them, wind ensembles offer audiences special works which contain unexpected beauty, and without which we would not have a clear and complete picture of Mozart.

Generally, these concerts take place in the morning, together with lectures and visits to museums and libraries, including an outstanding address that we heard given by Dr Goebbels. In the afternoon, the main items are chamber concerts: string quartets, etc. But it is at night that, for us, the most interesting elements of the festival take place. Certainly, we cannot figure out if they take place before or after dinner! This is something that we Spaniards find somewhat difficult, because we cannot face dinner at 6pm, and at 11pm, when the opera finishes, it is rather late to dine.

The opera performances coincide with some concerts of great interest, for example, by Backhaus, Edwin Fischer, or Gieseking, and because of this we harbour a little resentment towards the organisers, because we had to forego hearing some of them. Not Fischer – in order to hear him we ventured out to Schönbrunn, in absolutely freezing weather. Fischer abundantly repaid our sacrifice, giving us an interpretation of Mozart that was admirable in its simplicity and feeling.

But finally, we decided on the operas. Opera by Mozart! We Spaniards have so few opportunities to hear them. Opera is Mozart's dream, his ambition, it is his father's desire, and the constant element in Mozart's life. From *Die Entführung aus dem Serail* to *The Magic Flute*, by way of *Così fan tutte, The Marriage of Figaro, Don Giovanni* and *Idomeneo* – what wonders of harmony and beauty we are able to enjoy! Thus, in one opera after another, we can study how Mozart trained himself, by means of thousands of influences, and when his task is finished the inevitable and wondrous transformation has taken place. The greatest of Italian musicians, with some obvious French influences, stands before us as he really is: the master of German classical music. For this reason, it seems wrong to my mind to call Mozart an 'international' musician. He may seem so, at first sight, but getting to know him in depth shows that he is not – yet another of the paradoxes of Mozart's art.

I have deliberately left till last to comment, albeit very briefly, on the work of the real artists of this proud Mozart Week that Germany has put on so perfectly, in spite of current events. These artists are the conductors who have taken part in the series of concerts. We are indebted to Knappertsbusch for two conscientious performances of *The Magic Flute* and *Don Giovanni*. From Clemens Krauss there was a superb interpretation of the curious and interesting *Mass in C minor*, and a delightful performance of *Così fan tutte*, in which the conductor, Krauss, played the harpsichord with a lightness and elegance that took us back to those chamber concerts of the 18th century.

For his part, Karl Böhm offered us a Mozart which, as far as I am concerned, is the most authentic that we have heard, because of its elegance, its lightness and its surrealism. His *Die Entführung aus dem Serail* was already an indication of his qualities, and his performance of *The Marriage of Figaro* was the best of the operas given in the Hall of the Imperial Royal Palace. It remains, as I have said, the most perfect Mozart that we have heard.

These opera productions are supported by various casts in whom we see the cohesion and discipline that have made these model interpretations, even though there may not be at the moment any particularly outstanding singers.

Finally the 5th of December arrives, and the Mozart Week comes to an end, with the anticipated *Requiem*, conducted by Furtwängler. Here we run out of superlatives. To be able to control two hundred and fifty voices, an orchestra of almost one hundred players; to be able to obtain from that impressive mass such flexibility, lightness and balance; to shape it all with only a few gestures, is simply awesome. The performance of the *Requiem* by Furtwängler will stand as one of the six or seven musical highpoints of our lives.

Amongst the opera performances that I mentioned, there was one extremely interesting one. It was *Idomeneo*, the work that is the turning point in Mozart's music. This time there was extra interest, because the work was conducted by Richard Strauss. A few days ago he appeared in a box and was recognised by the whole audience, who stood to applaud him.

Germany has proved once more that its intellectual life is intact. Its musical life is more than intact, it is outstanding. This has been recognised by all the nations musically represented here, amongst which is France, with a delegation headed by Schmitt and Honegger.

Germany has received all its foreign guests – more than two hundred – with its marvellous and characteristic openness. For these few days we all felt at our ease, in a city which, musically speaking, has improved a great deal.

And so we leave Vienna with regret, the home of so many musicians, which has welcomed us with its lovely elegance during this unforgettable Mozart Week.

1942

The Salzburg Festival

Twenty barely remembered years separate my two stays in Salzburg. Superficially, Mozart's city has changed a great deal: cars, so many cars, motorcycles, lorries and jeeps, tell us of the triumph of tourism and of the motorcar, and confirm the presence of an army of occupation. But after this first impression, I find once again the Salzburg of 1935 where I spent two unforgettable months. At that time Salzburg was one of the few cities, indeed perhaps the only one, to organise festivals of music and drama. That seed germinated well throughout the world, and nowadays festivals have become a kind of enjoyable epidemic, from April to October, in cities large and small, with or without an artistic past, with or without a reason. But why not, after all? They work hard to follow the example of Salzburg, which focuses on Mozart. Salzburg today is Mozart, as Mozart was Salzburg. It is a good way to honour their son, perhaps the only way, by living through him. If you believed in determinism, you would say that Mozart could not have been born in any other city, this enclave between Italy and Germany, just as Mozart was the synthesis of German and Latin genius. Deep down, then, nothing has changed, not even those attractive Salzburg cafés which we discover again, with the same names as before, the same bars and restaurants, alongside the noisy, tumbling river Salzach which surrounds the city, as cheery as a Mozart symphony.

Not many hours pass before we hear the voice of an old friend: it is the cathedral carillon which, at 11 o'clock and 6 o'clock, pipes the minuet from *Don Giovanni*. This time, the operas that are available are fewer than that other, memorable occasion when I was here. Only two Mozart operas feature this season: *Così fan tutte* and *Don Giovanni*. I have to admit that I do not like *Così fan tutte*. Mozart is repeating himself, at a time in his life, during his later years, when genius wishes not to repeat itself. It gives the impression, immediately proved correct, that Mozart is searching for a different kind of music, the kind that he had already attempted in *Die Entfürung aus dem Serail*. But this was too soon. He needed to write *Don Giovanni* and, the crowning glory of Italian opera of the 18th century, *The Marriage of Figaro*. *Così fan tutte* is written without much thought. Mozart, though he did not know it, was already thinking of *The Magic Flute*. I accept that *Don Giovanni* does not achieve the perfection of *The Marriage of Figaro*, but I love this rather long play, full of comings and goings, rich in Italianate modes, and saturated from beginning to end in – no need to search for the term – genius.

This year Furtwängler has taken over, which assured us of a careful, correct version, more serious than light-hearted, with more attention paid to the music than to the production, which to my mind is not in accord with the spirit of Mozart. Furtwängler was never a Mozart man, and his slow tempi, already excessive in a really Germanic work like *Der Freischütz*, also part of the Festival, were far too evident in this performance of *Don Giovanni*. It was perfectly realised, on an enormous stage, with more than two hundred extras and with soloists of the first category: Elisabeth Schwarzkopf, as Donna Elvira, will be an abiding memory; Elisabeth Grümmer as Donna Ana, a gentler, less dramatic character. (She is better in the role of Agathe, in *Der Freischütz* – and what an Agathe! It would be difficult to hear the third act aria sung more beautifully, or in a sweeter voice). There was a good Don Giovanni and even a good Don Ottavio; a difficult role, this, disliked for some reason, but for which Mozart wrote some very beautiful arias. But the thing that draws the whole Festival together is the Vienna Philharmonic Orchestra, as good as ever, but in Strauss's *Ariadne auf Naxos* it excelled itself under the baton of Karl Böhm. A magnificent work which, were it not for this interpretation, would still be fairly tedious to listen to.

Added to this are concerts of all types, the presence of more than three hundred, almost four hundred, critics, teachers and students, who bring delight to the city, and who attend the Mozarteum. Salzburg is a summer city, and it comes alive under the spell of the Festivals. It has its Conservatoire, the Mozarteum, directed by Bernhard Paumgartner who has made Mozart's music, which he understands like no other, his life's work. At the Conservatoire we are delighted to find a teacher of violin who is a Spaniard, Filiberto Estrela – from Valencia, no less – and always ready to support our music, which is so noticeably absent from this and other festivals. If you don't believe this, let the recent festival in Santander prove it! How much contemporary Spanish music have foreign students been able to hear there, if any even attended? Only Falla, who can already be heard everywhere. However… to continue with Salzburg. Over the winter there are two orchestras, the municipal orchestra and the chamber orchestra from the Mozarteum, made up of the professors who are specialists in Mozart there.

Now, once again, it is time to leave Salzburg's cafés and comfortable sofas, to eat a last slice of pie and cream, listen to the last minuet on the carillon and promise, over a stein of beer, that another twenty years will not go by before we return to Salzburg.

1954

Beethoven, 'the Spaniard'

Almost two hundred years ago in Germany, in Bonn, an attractive town near Cologne, there came into the world, on the 16th December, as the snow was falling, a child who would become the greatest musician of all time. A man who would turn music into a limitless, universal art. This man was Ludwig van Beethoven.

His character, a mixture of rages and impetuosity, of delicacy and tenderness, made him write music in the way that mediaeval architects used to build their cathedrals: reaching to the hearts of men but feeling very near to God. They called him 'the Spaniard' because of his olive skin and deep, dark eyes. And, above all, because of his temperament – impulsive, daring and nothing like his compatriots.

Beethoven had to put up with a troublesome heritage, which influenced so much of the rest of his life. A consumptive mother, who would die young, and an alcoholic and abusive father, whose professed faith was that 'learning comes best with punishment'. He was obsessed by the example of the young Mozart who a few years before had passed through Bonn, amazing everybody with his improvisations and performances. He wanted to create another such in his son Ludwig, forcing him to practise for hours and hours on the spinet, even tying him to it on more than one occasion.

The Beethoven family house, which escaped so many bombings and still survives in Bonn, was, or rather, is, a garret of low ceilings and limited space. Here the parents, three or four children, instruments, scores, etc. were all piled in together. It was a sad house, intensely sad, only disturbed by the studies of the son or the regular shouts of the father who, after a day's work in the Archduke's chapel, would return home the worse for drink.

After a lot of problems, a lot of shouting and of punishment, Beethoven was becoming technically adept and had acquired a sufficient understanding of musical composition to allow him, still a child, to enter the service of the Prince Archduke, as organist. In this way he was able to contribute to the maintenance of his family with a wage that drink could not squander in quite so noticeable a way.

In this sad childhood and adolescence, there is some light. It is the kind and gentle light of the family home of the von Breunings, people from the best of Bonn society. Here, the young musician will become teacher to the children and, in a very short time, will be accepted as another of their sons. Beethoven teaches music to the daughter and receives in turn classes on behaviour and much-needed good manners. His character begins to develop: a bit taciturn, a little proud, with sudden and unexpected flashes of bad temper, even brief rages which sometimes cause him to leave that much-loved house to which he would always return with noble remorse. Soon he will experience his first love, finding himself irresistibly attracted to Leonora. Leonora loves Beethoven like a brother, and she makes him understand this. It is his first disillusion in love, but friendship with her and with her brother will last for the whole of his life. We know of the touching detail that, when Beethoven died, a yellowing letter from Leonora would be found in the pocket of an old jacket. In the letter a still adolescent Leonora tells him that she is sending him a scarf, made by herself, to stop him catching cold in freezing Vienna.

Beethoven settled finally in the Austrian capital after a variety of difficulties. His talent, indeed his originality, open the salons of important people to him, and his German uncouthness and provincial tastes adapt to the refinements of Viennese aristocracy. He begins to go about in society, he is almost elegant in his dress, he learns to ride and even goes so far as to take some dance lessons. He teaches in the best society, he is well received everywhere, he achieves great success as a pianist and conductor, but the terrible drama of his life is about to unfold. It will change his character, exacerbating and intensifying those innate aspects that have already been referred to. That drama – deafness.

He is barely twenty-five years old, and is just beginning to enjoy his first triumphs as a composer, when he begins to notice the early symptoms of what will become an inexorably progressive deafness. At first it is just buzzings, then noises. And, even worse for a musician, sounds become distorted. Beethoven is terrified. However, it is also one of the best times for him, as the beautiful Countess Giulietta comes into his life. Beethoven even forgets the illness that stalks him implacably, but the terrible and sudden abandonment of him by this beloved pupil, Giulietta, and the definitive worsening of his illness, plunge him into despair. He even tries to take his own life. He is now little more than thirty years old, and music is on the point of losing one of its greatest geniuses. But faith in his art and the conviction that he has something important to say make him abandon that idea.

Slowly, Beethoven draws apart from Viennese society. Little by little, he retires into himself, he becomes more withdrawn. But his music gains in inspiration, in depth. We can imagine how it must feel for a musician in full flood to find himself almost deprived of the faculty of hearing. Standing only a short distance from the orchestra, he cannot perceive its harmonies, and he confuses its sounds. Gradually, the illness gets worse and he ends up stone deaf. Beethoven shuts himself up in his house, once and for all. In his final years the few friends who visit him have to write down their questions and his replies; and thus we have the famous 'Conversation Notebooks'. Beethoven lives only for music. Though he has lost the ability to hear, his inner ear, fortunately, is even more acute. It is quite extraordinary that a musician who is completely deaf can extend, and in such a fashion, the sound-world of the piano, of the violin, and can create a new concept of the orchestra, one that is starting to learn how to describe, to paint pictures. The music of Beethoven, undoubtedly because of his intense concentration, because of the absolute silence around him, becomes full of a new, internal, imagery, drawn from the very depths of his being. He hears music in a strange, unearthly way; you could say that he 'contemplates' it, rather than hears it. From this comes his pleasure in counterpoint, in fugues, in the taut, almost ecstatic, dialogues of the quartet, in the interweaving of phrases. He sinks into, and draws out, the pure essence of themes in an exhaustive elaboration of form that comes from detailed investigation of a thematic formula. The last sonatas, the last quartets, are all a renunciation of life and love, all a surrendering of himself to his art, and, as a wonderful contrast, the Ninth Symphony, the greatest hymn to joy and love among men, who will one day love each other as brothers.

Whatever might have been the beauty of the music created by a Beethoven open to the outside world, there is no doubt it would not have achieved the same depths, nor the emotional beauty based on the serenity of contemplating the phenomenon of his inner hearing. In his work there is no guessing at sounds. He knows how to listen, and he hears the music from within, through a filter, for otherwise he could not have composed at all. But this remarkable gift modified his composing, changed his music, and his message became different, coming to us from afar. Almost from another world.

1970

'A Day in the Life of Beethoven'

The social transformations in Vienna at the start of the 19th century, Beethoven's age and his maladies, together with his disappointments and the gradual disappearance of friends and protectors, also change his way of life. Now, at forty, he is interested only in his work and his music. Here is how he spends a day of his life in the Austrian capital, in 1816, before the ill-fated idea of setting up home occurs to him.

Doctor Bursy (a doctor who apparently woke up very early) gives the following account: 'I found the master at seven in the morning seated at his work-desk, a piece of ruled paper in front of him, preparing his glass, cone-shaped coffee-maker.' This confirms the notes in Beethoven's diary, which read 'I study from half past five in the morning until breakfast time.' And his friend Schindler confirms that this is what he did at all times and seasons of the year, adding 'He would count the coffee beans until he had exactly sixty', which might perhaps appear extravagant to good housewives today, and goes on 'He would do this with minute care, even when he made coffee for his friends.'

He would work until two or three, his lunchtime. He interrupted his work, apparently, to go out into the street two or three times. This was a necessity. During these excursions, in which he continued composing, neither cold nor heat would bother him, and he would even spend an hour wandering around without caring where he went. This intense work, both intellectual and physical, gave the master a more than normal appetite, and so it was not uncommon to see him at those times enter *The Swan* or *The Pear* rapidly and thirstily. Two or three good swallows of wine comforted both body and spirit, and then, it is said, he would try up to three different soups until he found the one he liked best. He was, nevertheless, neither fussy nor difficult. He would say to Fani del Río (we will return one day to this humble friend with the Spanish name), 'It's pointless to eat more than our bodies need!'

The time for his favourite dish would arrive: macaroni with delicious Parma cheese, and a fine sturgeon, just caught in the Danube, with potatoes, which he would accompany with a good Hungarian wine (which he preferred to all others), in spite of it being rather 'prepared'. Nevertheless his favourite drink was always fresh water, which he consumed in vast quantities, to the point of being reprimanded by his brother Johann. In the afternoons he would go for walks – the time for his daily and regular excursions. In the evenings he would go into his accustomed tavern to leaf through the newspapers and mutter to himself. The long winter nights he almost always spent at home reading, very rarely writing, as this tired his eyesight. Reading inspired him, and in those first hours of the night he enjoyed going to bed and creating the themes and melodies of his works. The nearby bell towers would strike ten and then Beethoven would retire. Seven or eight hours were sufficient for him to rest, and the following day he would take up his life of regular and methodical work again, into which an amusing character would soon intrude – rather unfortunately. His maid.

1944

Beethoven and his Servants

In our delight at the immortal creations of great artists we never think that these works could have been interrupted and even menaced by apparently trivial things, and by insignificant people who passed through their lives, leaving no historical trace. In the case of Beethoven it can be affirmed without exaggeration that maids, cooks and servants have deprived us of more than one sonata, and even of symphonies.

———

'When I am ill I need different relationships with people. And as far as getting a maidservant, I'll think about it. If I was not absolutely convinced of the total corruption of the Austrian state, I might hope to find an honourable person, and everything would be easy, but...!'

Beethoven wrote this to Frau Streicher, the wife of the famous piano manufacturer, a very good friend, who was his domestic adviser, landlady and confidante. But in spite of doubts, omens and suspicions towards this class of people, 'the most discredited of all', there follows a series of tragicomic letters, in which he communicates his decision, amid vacillations and protests – 'This Congress of Vienna has almost corrupted us and filled the old servant class with vices' – to establish a home where he can have his 'beloved son Karl' (the dear little nephew who would turn out to be such a dubious character) and engage a maid and cook for them both.

The good lady, even though a little alarmed, finally offers him two acceptable examples: Nanni, 'with the opulent body', and Baberi, 'the beautiful villain' (Beethoven himself describes them thus). Both are rather dim, which is always a consolation, and because of this and other mischiefs, Nanni, with her good looks, is abruptly dismissed soon afterwards, and 'the beautiful villain' receives a substantial Christmas present, consisting of half a dozen heavy books thrown at her head, with a verbal dismissal in language which was not exactly classical.

'Something of this must have entered her evil heart and her brain, because since then she has changed a lot', he writes to his confidante (she had either learnt a hard lesson, or the roguish beauty of Baberi made him find her more acceptable). The girls, for their part, accept these chastisements, which are known about everywhere; innocent scoldings, but they exasperated the famous composer, just as they exasperate present-day housewives. They went round the neighbourhood discrediting our colossus with a hotchpotch of fabrications, inventions and truths. Frau Streicher was terrified – if only she had not got involved! – but anything for music, and for her admired and venerated master. The following anecdote proves how difficult it was, given the character of Beethoven and his extreme concept of honour, to find servants for him. Having asked him why he had dismissed another girl, who was otherwise good and who had only, in order not to offend him, told an unimportant white lie, Beethoven replied adamantly: 'Anyone who lies does not have a pure heart, and such a person cannot prepare a wholesome soup!'

Finally, in spite of these uninspiring beginnings, on the 24th January 1818 his nephew Karl is brought to the house, a tutor is appointed, and he goes in search of a good servant once more. Again the good offices of his friend bring him Peppi, 'the cook Peppi, who prepares food well', which makes the master extremely grateful to his domestic protector, and, thanks to the new girl, some sort of order enters the house. 'With God's help I will now be able to devote myself entirely to my art...' Beethoven will devote himself to his art thanks to this particular Peppi. But this happiness was not to last long, since it is very unwise to trust 'Peppis', no matter how well they cook...

Beethoven's 'Pastoral' Symphony

In that spring of 1808 the birds were singing more beautifully, the violets were a more silken blue, and their perfume was more penetrating. Was it really so? Would it not have been the hands of Teresa Malfatti as she picked them, and her laughter as she pulled off the petals, under the fir trees? And the brook too was sparkling more brightly, that brook of which Beethoven would write 'the stronger its current, the deeper its voice'. In the spring of 1808 Beethoven at last feels happy. And this almost child-like happiness, inspired by the fragile dreams and distant hopes in which only the continually inflamed soul of that genius can believe, creates this 'Pastoral' Symphony, which Beethoven writes, wandering alone or in the company of that attractive young girl, Teresa - she who, without any sense of the greatness of her companion, leads him to conceive plans which will never be realised.

Because all this is present, one could even say 'sensed', in this music; because on hearing it, it is as though the sunny landscape of Heiligenstadt is spread before us, and we see the groups of village musicians pass by and the country people gather around him, making this Symphony all the more delightful. We have greater admiration for the Fifth and the Ninth, we are more disturbed by the 'Eroica', and feel a greater excitement in the Seventh; but our deepest affection and tenderness will always be reserved for the 'Pastoral' Symphony. Yet beneath its innocent surface there lies hidden the daring of a musician who knows himself to be above not just musical formulas, but concepts.

Today it can seem the most natural thing in the world that a symphony's 'andante' should be called 'Scene by the brook', but then it implied – as later the appearance of choirs in the Ninth Symphony would – first, the complete mastery of the symphony, and second, a new conception arising not only from emotion but from the deepest reflection. In spite of everything, even though Beethoven knew his own strength, and was aware of his symphonic reach and the strictly musical aims of his work, he had to shelter himself from his own storm with the careful lightning-conductor of his 'more an expression of feeling than painting'. It was only this famous phrase, printed at the head of the score, which would mitigate the real storm which was aroused by the audacity of substituting joyful feelings for 'allegros', idylls for 'adagios', and country dances for 'scherzos'.

But, nevertheless, nothing of this was completely new, and Beethoven had possibly seen something similar. Similar? Yes. As we can read in Chantavoine, a poor devil named Knecht, twenty-four years before Beethoven's 'Pastoral' Symphony, had published another 'pastoral symphony' in 1784, whose music – of the most insignificant and banal kind – attempted to respond to the following stimuli: 'A musical portrait of nature, or great symphony... which it will depict through sounds'; 1) 'a beautiful spot where the sun shines and the breezes waft...'; 2) 'the sky suddenly darkens...'; 3) 'the storm, accompanied by howling winds and furious rain, roars with all its force...'; 4) 'the storm gradually abates...'; 5) 'Nature, full of joy, raises its voice to the heavens...'.

This work, from the same publishing house as the one where not long afterwards three of the young Beethoven's Sonatinas would appear, must have struck the acute sensibilities of the young man as the failed promise of amusing musical possibilities; and those titles would reappear twenty-four years later within the following almost identical ones, written by that same adolescent who was now fully mature: 'Joyous feelings on arriving in the country', 'Scene by the brook', 'Happy gathering of country folk', 'Storm', 'Shepherd's hymn'; 'feelings of happiness and fulfilment after the storm'. But Beethoven neither wishes, nor knows, nor can believe in the power or in the real pictorial value of music, and makes his opinion clear when he writes: 'in order to 'paint', I prefer painting'. This is why he insists: 'rather an expression of feeling than of painting'. Thus we would go astray if we were to see a real, an actual sunlit landscape of Heiligenstadt spread before us, and a group of village musicians crossing it, coming together finally with the other country people in order, all together – as in the most flimsy operas – to sing a hymn of thanks to the Creator. There is something more than all this, there is the escape to nature from the Classicism which had forgotten it, the influence of new emotions which appear in music via Jean-Jacques Rousseau, and in addition, that subjectivity which is brought into the objective forms of music, which, after the superhuman perfection of the Fifth Symphony, might have remained cold and inert.

It is astonishing to think of the creative power of Beethoven. Remember, for example, that these two Symphonies were composed simultaneously, and that it was in fact the Sixth which was the first to be completed, and might well have been given the number 'Five'. Twin creations, then, and nevertheless, if two works by the same composer could be totally unlike each other, they would be the Fifth and Sixth Symphonies. Beethoven was in a hurry to finish the 'Pastoral'; one might say that he was afraid of not being able to do it, knowing that the birds would soon stop singing, that the violets would die even more quickly, and that even in Austria the streams can go dry, and an idyll beside them would become impossible.

In that same year, at the famous concert given on the 22nd December which inspired the well-known group of Beethoven's friends to resolve to give him a sum of money to prevent him having to leave Vienna permanently – a group which would not stay together for long – at that famous concert, the Fifth and Sixth Symphonies were performed for the first time, in the same programme.

Let us look at the music of the 'Pastoral'. In the first place, as we have seen, Beethoven introduces new and even disturbing elements into the aesthetic concept of the symphony. He breaks the traditional four-movement form and introduces another movement, the fifth, the storm. On the other hand, the 'Pastoral' does not end with the traditional 'allegro' or 'presto', but rather, with two rapid or agitated movements having preceded the last movement – the 'scherzo' and the storm – he ends with a serenely happy movement in which, for the first time, the variation form appears as a means of developing the themes of a final movement. The clarinet and the horn are heard and the variations skip after them; whereas the orchestra, less happily than in the rest of the Symphony because of a certain undeniable heaviness, caused by the great string figures, supported by dense woodwind chording, rather blurs the richness of the themes.

Before this the storm has broken out, the clouds are torn apart, and the thunder has rolled. This is without doubt the most original part of the work. Never before in the symphony, or since, had such expressive force appeared, and perhaps never again would a storm be depicted – yes, why not say 'depicted'? – with fewer resources and with more musicality. The means employed are simple, but there is not a single expressive element here which is not used so carefully that we do not feel we are still within the bounds of Classicism. We can look in vain for an accumulation of sound, cacophony or onomatopoeia; all that is necessary is a series of staccato notes in the strings, extremely expressive ascending progressions, string tremolos, and a drum roll, for the emotion and the fearfulness of the storm to strike us. Beethoven in fact utilises normal resources and uses the diminished seventh chord – disturbing both before him and indeed afterwards – upon which the storm breaks out, and the clouds descend in shreds, caught by the descending accents of the violins. The storm passes, and a final lightning-flash crosses the orchestral air on the wings of a luminous flute.

Before this the peasants have danced in delight, and Beethoven himself with them, because it is good to enjoy beautiful days before storms destroy our dreams. In this 'scherzo' the composer has enjoyed imitating – so skilfully and calmly – the happy gatherings of country musicians and their dances. This happiness, which an almost imperceptible distant roll of thunder will break, has been preceded by an admirable movement, the beautiful scene by the brook. Listen to how the orchestra murmurs, in an evocation of the gentle flow of the stream, in a brilliant orchestral depiction which Wagner would use in a more developed form, much later, for when Siegfried awakes to a life of love, hearing the sounds of the forest. And see how the most tender and passionate theme which Beethoven ever wrote gently emerges. In the incredible, and richest, collection of melodies which any composer has left us – undoubtedly Beethoven's – we will not find another theme like this. The violins and clarinet play in dialogue and above and below that dialogue, like the perfect canopy and softest bed, the birds sing and the brook murmurs as it passes. Suddenly all is silent, the lark sings, the cuckoo replies and the quail trills, and the chorus of aesthetic critics is in turmoil! What? Simple imitations of birdsong in the noble purity of a symphony? Beethoven, in this happy year of his life, is enjoying himself, and believes that he is in love, and is loved.

Finally, or rather in this case, to start with – because we have tried to give a brief summary of the Symphony in reverse – following Beethoven's memories fifteen years later, in that nostalgic conversation with Schindler on the day they return together to the very place where the 'Pastoral' was composed, that joy returns which inspired the popular tone of the first movement. In this splendid movement, a procedure which is unusual in Beethoven is begun, a development not by reduction but by repetition, something which would eventually be taken to great lengths. See how it modulates by fits and starts, how the harmony remains static, while above it simple melodic themes appear which are continuously and joyfully repeated. They seem like those momentary and happy pauses which we make as we walk in the country, when we turn our heads the better to look at the view, and which we remember as special places along the way. This movement is thus conceived as a wonderful movement forwards. The whole 'Pastoral' Symphony is bathed in this sense of nature, containing the purest and most quintessential essence of what 'popular' music should be.

The years would pass and with them springtime would embellish the fields of Vienna with flowers, and the sky would be filled with birdsong. Beethoven will return to Heiligenstadt, but he will not hear birdsong any more, neither in his ears nor in his heart. That does not matter – we will go on hearing it, for ever.

Beethoven's Enigmatic Friend

What an indescribable commotion shook the ancient walls of the Imperial Palace in Schönbrunn on that historic day in 1809. Excited comings and goings of the servants, anxious curiosity on the faces of the courtiers, lengthy, sibilant whisperings from the royal ladies which outdo the twittering of the birds... Napoleon has made his entrance into Schönbrunn, and another empire has fallen to the Corsican's irresistible advance.

Bonaparte is in a good mood and the courtiers, less anxious now, talk to the Emperor about the obsession of the Viennese at that time with the latest man of magic. The door of the small salon opens and a man, of some forty years and simply dressed, comes in. Behind him some servants drag towards the Emperor a heavy box, inside which is a chess board and, in amongst a jumble of levers, springs, screws, cylinders and ball bearings, sits an automaton, a life-like 'Turk', smoking a long pipe.

'Is this the prodigy?'

'Yes, your Majesty. My beloved Turk has beaten all the chess players who have dared to test themselves against his invincible brain: Frederick of Prussia, the Empress Marie Thérèse, the Emperor Francis, and he'll beat...'

'Splendid,' replies Napoleon, amused and intrigued. 'A new victory, even if over a Turk with a pipe, won't come amiss.' The game begins.

The inventor places himself beside his automaton and has on his knees a small, mysterious box which he touches or bangs from time to time. No wire or tube links that box with the contraption where the automaton plays impassively, with stiff, rhythmical movements. Napoleon moves his pawns somewhat suspiciously. The mysterious little man has impressed him, and that old Jacobite, who believes in neither God nor the Devil, knows that some ingenious device is hidden within the box, which he eagerly tries to guess at. He looks more at the automaton than the chessboard. He's distracted, he hesitates. 'Checkmate!' cries the figure, and the whisperings of the court ladies fly about deliriously – the Emperor has lost the game!

This first person to conquer Napoleon was a friend of Beethoven. He tried in vain to help his deafness by attempting to adjust several instruments and ear trumpets which merely served to keep grumpy Beethoven's hopes alive. Johann Nepomuk Maelzel was born in Regensburg in 1772. A clever musician and a brilliant mechanic, he was an outlandish, nervy type, part charlatan, part genius, a perennial mountebank. His life was a series of marvellous and incredible adventures, and his inventions and lies caused a commotion in nearly all the courts of his time. He loved to amaze, with his absurd inventions and 'happenings', those Enlightened times which, all unthinking, still believed in witches and spells.

His automaton trumpeter, which all on its own was able to sound the most military of bugle calls, became famous. His amazing workshop recalled those of legendary magicians and enchanters. Complicated mechanisms would make doors open and close before the fascinated gaze of visitors who, if they were unfortunate enough to sit in one of the comfortable armchairs, found they had been covered over and imprisoned within it, until the magician, laughing, came to rescue them. If a beautiful lady settled down on the sofa, as soon as she sat down a mysterious spring would be released and well-known, attractive music, as though from crystalline bells, would greet her ears.

With a head full of ideas, and his pockets empty, he thought: why not get something out of the friendship and prestige of Beethoven by putting together the composer's music with his extraordinary inventions, and make them both rich? After all, had he not got all those illustrious simpletons open-mouthed at his machinery? Had he not exploited Haydn's good nature with his wonderful, mechanised scene in which *The Seasons* had been represented with a great device to make storms and blizzards?

'Maestro, you must write a composition for my latest invention, my amazing mechanical orchestra, which will immortalise us and make us rich. No more musicians who groan about your difficult music, who do not understand your genius. My wonderful automata will be the caring and tireless heralds of your fame.' Saying this, he showed Beethoven, who was always amused by the chattering genius, his so-called *panharmonicon* (that really was a pretty good name for it!). It was an instrument that made sounds by means of a cylinder and a pair of bellows, with a goodly

71

number of jolly automata playing their instruments, directed by a conductor with his infallible baton. Beethoven, penniless but entertained by the toy, agreed.

An opportunity soon presented itself, in January, 1813, when news came of the Battle of Vitoria, when Napoleon lost again. Beethoven wrote *Wellington's Victory* for Napoleon's foremost conqueror, and it was premièred together with the Seventh Symphony, a strange combination which today would seem a heresy. All who stood for something in the world of music in Vienna at the time took part in that absurd concert: Hummel played the drum, Spohr the second violin, etc.

Beethoven's fame spread rapidly through Europe. What he could not achieve with his Symphonies and Sonatas was achieved by those simple automata and the wizardry of Maelzel. What was never achieved was the promised wealth, at least not for Beethoven. Maelzel would later sell his *panharmonicon* in America for a fabulous sum of money, and his invention survives to the present day. Before that, he travelled the world with his *orchestrion* and poor Beethoven's music. His huge income was wasted on extravagant banquets and a lavish life-style. His amazing 'Turk' would also remain in America, where it was lost in a fire, but not before it was discovered that, before the game started, that rogue Maelzel would hide an expert chess player inside the box. Certainly he was not invincible, but the other players, dazzled by the movements of the pipe-smoking Turk and Maelzel's glib manipulation of the small box, would be distracted and make wrong moves, which were seized on by the hidden player. Who took care never to offer return matches!

This extraordinary man, Maelzel, the last of the magicians, died in 1838, during his return from America, but not before playing on us musicians the last of his tricks – the invention of the metronome, that little pyramid which would immortalise his name and which we all have sitting on the piano, for our greater discomfort!

Maelzel had come to a lasting understanding of movement and of rhythm, unfortunately for us, and in his little pyramid box he imprisoned time.

1944

Beethoven: Life and Love

Beethoven's love-life, which we will try to summarise in the following notes, was not, in relation to women, a series of failures, as might initially appear the case, but was in fact a succession of impossibilities.

Music and love filled the life of this genius, the former sustaining him, guiding him, maintaining him upright against every adversity, raising him even above his fate; the latter illuminating the bitter grandeur of his solitude with brilliance – fleeting, it is true, but dazzling. Without any doubt he was the musician who loved the most, and who was also loved in return. But how was Beethoven loved? What kind of passion did he inspire?

His infancy was sad and bitter, his childhood without joy, almost without play, dark and gloomy like the house in which he was born, that house at Bonngasse 382, in the town of Bonn, where a man of good height could hardly enter, but which would serve to shelter a colossus. A father who was an unrepentant drunkard, a man of anger and of dreadful habits, a musician by chance. A mother who was sweet, but passive, poorly educated, and unwell. Between harshness and softness, barbarous treatments to make the boy emulate Mozart, and excessive pampering and abandonment, the child grew up unsociable, rebellious and wild. This inheritance and education, this example and predestination, formed from his early years on his hypersensitive personality an unhealthy inclination which made him fall into those 'fits', as his best friends would later call them.

The life of young Ludwig changes, nevertheless. One day (he is twelve, and they are already speaking about him at court) he is taken by one of the very few friends of the family, Franz Ries, to the von Breuning house. He is soon accepted as a child of the family, in which the absence of the father – a councillor at court who had died in a fire – made the influence of the mother on her four children all the more notable. She was an educated and intelligent woman, and had three boys, and a girl of approximately the same age as Beethoven. They belonged to the most ancient aristocracy of the country, and their position was comfortable. Inherited good taste, especially for music and an enjoyment of and inclination towards all kinds of artistic activity made an enchanted world of that atmosphere, something very special for the formation of an artist. Stefan, the third of the children, became an excellent violinist, and he would be the dedicatee, many years later, of the famous Violin Concerto. The girl was two years younger than Beethoven, and was called Leonora.

Young Ludwig is very quickly considered a child of the house. He spends whole days and weeks there, and when summer comes, he goes with the family to the castle of an uncle and aunt, that castle where everything is delightful. The influence of these childhood friends will be decisive on Beethoven. With them he learns not only good manners, but something more precious, the beginnings of a morality which would become the norm of his future conduct.

In the 18th century childhood was short. In addition, the years of adolescence passed without being noticed. Leonora, almost suddenly, appeared before the astonished eyes of Beethoven as a woman. Delicate, slender, graceful, she would occupy an important place in his life during his entire early youth, and perhaps beyond. We must suppose that essentially she did not understand Beethoven's genius, and would not have felt more than friendship and admiration for him, while what sprang up in the boy's heart was a deep love, which, in spite of not being returned, remained strong enough to stay with him throughout his entire life.

What could have occurred between Leonora and Beethoven? Doubtless a moment of untimely jealousy, a sudden and unexpected declaration and recriminations in which Beethoven's famous bad temper broke out for the first time, one of his 'fits'. Only one person could have known what happened, and told us, in addition, what Leonora was like. That person was Wegeler, a friend of both from infancy, and a constant friend and later biographer of Beethoven. Leonora would marry him at the age of thirty, an almost accepted age for the time. This late marriage to a man with whom she had been intimate from childhood perhaps explains the character of Leonora, possibly cold, reserved and timid. For an uncertain but practical woman, accustomed to being the object of fuss and flattery from three brothers and a widowed mother, Beethoven's desires must have seemed madness – and anyway he was going to Vienna to study and make a name for himself. She therefore marries the long-established friend who lives in the same town, but only when her mother has become elderly and the family has possibly broken up. But Wegeler is happy enough to publish two letters, without which this first love of Beethoven's would have remained forgotten.

The first, dated in Vienna on the 2nd November 1793, says amongst other things:

> Respected Leonora and dearest friend: I have been here in the capital for almost a year and you are only now receiving a letter from me, even though the memory of you remains as clear to me as ever. I have often thought of you and your family, but it is just that I have often lacked the necessary tranquillity that I would have needed. My mind would dwell on that awful argument, and my behaviour then seemed so hateful. But the deed was done, and what I would not have given to be able to erase completely from my life my disgraceful conduct, which is so unlike my true character... And to finish, my dear friend, may I allow myself a request? It would make me so happy to receive an angora jacket, woven by your hands. Please forgive this temerity. It is due to my predilection for everything which comes from your hands, and I can tell you secretly – something really rather presumptuous – that I should like to be able to say that I possess something made by one of the best and most admirable girls in Bonn...

Leonora not only forgave everything that had occurred, but, acceding to her friend's request, sent him a present which gave rise to the beautiful letter which begins: 'I was extremely surprised to receive the beautiful scarf made by you. It awoke feelings of sadness in me, in spite of being such a lovely thing. It reminded me of that past time, making me ashamed at the noble attitude you have taken towards me. Truly, I did not think that you would deign to remember me.' And it ends: 'Goodbye, dear friend; it is not possible for me to call you anything else; and even though it may be a matter of indifference to you, I assure you that I esteem you as much as before, and your mother too. Think occasionally of this friend who reveres you so...'

With these words, full of hidden love and bitter resignation, the great man falls silent. The passion which had burnt in his heart during his entire adolescence becomes purified, without losing any of its initial intensity, and when he dies, a note is found in his wallet, dated 1782. A simple little note of congratulation from Leonora, surrounded by a garland of dried flowers – those flowers which had retained for Beethoven the perfume of his first love.

Fernando Sor on the 2nd Centenary of his Birth
The early years of the guitar

Although as early as the 14th century the Arcipreste de Hita mentions the Latin guitar and the Moorish guitar in his *Libro de buen amor*, it is not until the end of the 16th century that the guitar is fully naturalised in Spain, with the publication in Barcelona of the manual for guitar by Dr Amat. At this point the guitar begins to spread, especially in the hands of barbers and humble travelling musicians. Then it is necessary to wait until the second half of the 17th century for the book on the guitar by Gaspar Sanz, who was musician and courtier to the second Juan de Austria. After that, it was another century before encountering Fernando Sor, in the full flood of Classicism.

He was an extraordinary guitarist, travelling throughout Europe, including Russia, and his many works raised the guitar into the same category as other concert instruments. Sonatas, études, *fantasías*, variations, etc. are marvellous enrichments of the literature of our instrument and they remain, unchanged, in the repertoire of all guitarists to this day. At first, Sor's music depended on Mozart and Beethoven. But his compositions are intrinsically guitaristic, though drawn from classic harmonies and melodic inspiration, and, in fact, would not be bettered until modern composers began to take an interest in, and to write for, the guitar in its established form of six strings, after many changes and modifications.

Two hundred years have passed and his music remains with us, classic in concept, classic in form and composition. It is a product of its time and has a musicality that is both refined and individual.

1978

Carl Maria von Weber's *Oberon*

Carl Maria von Weber's leap to fame is based on three works known throughout the world: *Der Freischütz, Euryanthe* and *Oberon*. More than a century has passed since the emotional thoughts and Romantic ideas of Weber were transferred to the page, and yet all the luxuriance of that epoch breathes with the freshness of those times, when the woods of Germany were full of fairies, and the moon and the wind talked to them.

Oberon was first performed in London in 1826, shortly before the composer died. The work is inspired by the feelings that abound in German literature in the first years of the 19th century, that age when the first markers are put down for the links between the artist, his own passions and the natural world. This gradually allowed the doors to open to Romanticism, which some years later would achieve its dazzling heights.

The rustle of branches in the endless expanses of fir trees, mixed with the slow, unchanging flow of German rivers ('neither stopping nor hurrying', as Goethe said of his stars); the solitariness which surrounds the mediaeval castles like a floating garment, all form part of Weber's *Oberon*. Weber is one of the musicians who was best able to represent his nation's poetry in sound, which was then launched to the four winds as the definitive characteristic of the deepest and most subtle of German compositions.

The book *Oberon*, which Weber set to music, belongs to the fantasy genre of German ballads, and the call of the Elf on his horn enhances his character in the minds of romantic spirits, so that he becomes a veritable symphonic giant to the minds of those who follow him in the 19th century.

Felix Mendelssohn's *The First Walpurgis Night*

It was only natural that a Romantic composer like Mendelssohn, even if he tended more to Classicism, should be attracted to the famous 'Walpurgis Night'. This topic, together with a procession of witches and covens, would broaden the descriptive possibilities of music and greatly enrich the orchestral palette. Berlioz, in his *Symphonie Fantastique*, was the first composer to describe a terrifying witches' sabbath, followed later by Liszt and even by Saint-Saëns who, though there was little of the Romantic in him, was born at the height of Romanticism, as is evident in his, I would dare to call 'elegant', *Danse macabre*, and his symphony, based on the 'Dies irae'. For its part, opera was not slow with this theme, beginning with the terrifying scene in the second act of *Der Freischütz*, followed by macabre cemeteries and processions, with Mephistopheles and a few lesser, more or less agreeable devils.

Mendelssohn's approach to Walpurgis Night was an impeccably restrained presentation of the theme, rather than something dependent on the satanic.

Mendelssohn's friendship with Goethe dates from the memorable occasion when, at only 12 years old, his teacher Zelter took Mendelssohn to see him. *The First Walpurgis Night* is the most important of his compositions based on Goethe's poetry. For those who associate it primarily with the oratorio, it may be surprising to know that the poem tells of a reunion of pagans and druids, who meet to celebrate the classic gathering on the night of Walpurgis, disguised as devils in order to frighten off the intrusive Christians. In spite of this, Mendelssohn used to say that he was inspired to write the work by the musical gatherings organised by his sister, Fanny Hensel, on Sundays. It was a favourite work amongst the family members, and the last music heard by Fanny, who died while conducting a rehearsal of it.

Influenced perhaps by Haydn's *The Seasons*, Mendelssohn begins the work with a long, instrumental overture, entitled 'A violent storm'. Its principal theme is similar to the one that opens the slow introduction of the *Scottish Symphony*, begun at approximately the same time. But the nature of each is very different; what seems taciturn and melancholy in the Symphony appears here expressed with the greatest energy. The stormy atmosphere lasts for a long time, sometimes gloomy and mysterious, and more often fierce and violent, with a constantly crackling tension brought about by fast passages of semiquavers. There are various energetic climaxes, one of which is marked 'triple forte', something that occurs very rarely in Mendelssohn. After such sustained vigour, the transition to calmer music comes about very gradually, but, in due course the sad, wintry atmosphere gives way to music of glorious, spring-like freshness, entitled 'Transition towards Spring'. After a few bars, which curiously foreshadow a passage in the first movement of Brahms's Second Symphony, the first clarinet plays a phrase which gradually comes to the fore and is later sung by the tenor soloist, 'May is in full bloom'. These two ideas are given a serene, gentle treatment and, after the tenor and choir enter, the music continues like this for a time. But towards the end, when there is mention of sacrificial burnings to come, the pace picks up. The word 'hinauf' ('upwards') is repeated so much that it would have irritated the Major-General in *The Pirates of Penzance!*, but the music in itself has real fire and urgency.

In the next movement an old woman warns the pagans about the punishments they can expect if the Christians capture them. Perhaps surprisingly, this section is not headed by a familiar Mendelssohn notation – 'agitato' – which is probably why it starts in a rather uncertain stillness. The music is very serene, and only on occasions does it reach 'forte'. With all its restraint and economy of notes it gives rise to a powerful sensation of foreboding. By the middle of the movement the chorus enters, but the final bars are sung by the contralto soloist. In music that at first is very dignified and then rather martial, the druid priest encourages the pagans, assuring them that the woods will protect them by offering them refuge. Then, in a short and lively chorus, the pagans disperse to various places in the forest to mount guard. After this comes a phrase sung by the tenor at the beginning of the next chorus. It is deliciously clear and delicate, though the atmosphere is perhaps a little too like *A Midsummer Night's Dream* to be entirely appropriate to this situation.

This cannot be said of the music that follows. In a short recitative, a druid sentry suggests that they should all disguise themselves as devils, and this leads into what is undoubtedly the most impressive part of the work. The sentry takes control at the beginning of 'Come with prongs and pitchforks', a cautious marching rhythm, the tenors and basses of the chorus come together, and the orchestral accompaniment, very pared down to start with, grows increasingly lively, with sinister calls from the woodwind. The next movement begins with a sudden and brilliant modulation from G to A minor, where the same words are sung, but this time by the entire chorus. Here the music is very far indeed from the delicacy suitable for a fairy tale; it races along in rapid sixths and octaves, occasionally interrupted by two bars of 2/4 time. This pulse continues in the climax, and the phrases played by the woodwind in the previous movements return with even greater ferocity. Once the tumult has calmed down, the voice of the druid priest is heard again and, after an agitated movement where the flight of the terrified Christians is described, it is his music which provides the final word.

Berlioz's opinion of this work is fully justified: 'a masterpiece of Romanticism'.

1981

Hector Berlioz

This year the musical world is commemorating the centenary of the death of the first of the musicians of the constellation of the Romantics – Hector Berlioz – who died on the 8th March 1869, in Paris.

He was born in 1803 in a picturesque little village, La Côte St André, in the Département of Isère. His father was a doctor, a refined man and much attracted to music. His mother, who was exceptionally beautiful, suffered from the affliction of the century – melancholia. There wasn't a single musical instrument in the house, indeed music was hardly heard at all in that tranquil spot, except for church services on Sundays, and also that of a very modest quartet of enthusiasts, who could hardly manage to get to grips with even the simplest works of Haydn. In this atmosphere, full of uncertain Haydn, young Hector, who got carried away by the little music that he did manage to hear, learnt to play the flute, and applied himself to the guitar, which he came to play very well and which must have been very useful in his early, rather bohemian, years.

His very first steps at composing are intuitive, and astonish the few enthusiasts around him – his father and those four selfless and, as it were empirical, quartet players. But his father wanted him to study medicine, and sent him to Paris. Berlioz began his studies with absolutely no enthusiasm; but soon he enrolled in the Conservatoire, putting up with tirades and diatribes from his parents, so beginning a difficult existence that would last for several years.

It has been said of Berlioz that his studies in music at the Conservatoire and, therefore, his musical education, were very deficient. Not at all. His two teachers, Reicha and Lesueur, were among the best qualified in the Conservatoire, and they fought to keep both themselves and their students free from the tyrannical influence of the Italian music of that time. Also, and this is the most important and significant aspect of the high quality of his training, Berlioz was soon to win the most valued and prestigious prize of the Paris Conservatoire: the *Prix de Rome*. This prize, which still exists, as it also exists in Spain, meant not only the possibility of spending a few years in the Eternal City but also the culmination of his musical studies and his recognition as a scholar with a truly comprehensive technical knowledge. The prize was the supreme ambition of all students of composition. On his return from Rome he settled permanently in Paris, and so began the years of struggle and of incomprehension on the part of the public and the majority of musicians.

Around 1830, Paris was more or less completely given over to Italian opera. Very little remained of the great tradition of French opera, and the memory of its great masters of the Baroque, organists and harpsichordists, had almost disappeared. Rossini's operas, with their easy, cheerful, comic music, and their sentimental but high quality 'bel canto', swept across Europe and triumphantly stormed the one remaining outpost of symphonic music, Vienna. Paris acclaimed the Italian master at the height of his glory. And Meyerbeer's star was rising over the Parisian horizon with its train of more and more operas, composed from a clever mix of light Italian, French and German music, accompanied by an infallible sense of theatre, and by an orchestra which was beginning to be noted for what would become the new Romantic concept of instrumental colour.

Berlioz's unusual nature would be in total conflict with all this. He immediately takes the side of the Romantic movement, of which he is the first in time, heading a group of musicians with names like Mendelssohn, Schumann, Chopin, Liszt, Wagner and Verdi. Musicians who would bring in a new age that could already be heard, unmistakably, in the last works of Beethoven, the operas of Weber, and the poetic musical world of Schubert.

The first clarion call of real Romantic music sounds, or better still, thunders out in Paris in 1830 with the first performance of Berlioz's masterpiece, the *Symphonie Fantastique*. Berlioz is twenty-seven years old, so it is not too soon for a Romantic musician. Confronted by that new sound, the musical world is disconcerted, even stupefied, not realising that the young composer has just laid the foundations of French symphonic music, and established a new, virtually unknown, concept of instrumental colour. Whatever may have been the supremacy of the orchestral writing of the Vienna School, absolute though it was, Haydn and Mozart were indifferent to the individuality of instrumental timbre – its 'personality', as it were. Only Beethoven, in his 'Pastoral' Symphony or his Ninth Symphony, together with the orchestra in Weber's final operas, sense the particular character of each one of the instruments that comprise the Classical orchestra. But Berlioz invents colour when he discovers the unique personality that the distinctive sound of each instrument communicates. From this will arise a whole new expressiveness, to which Romanticism, with all its legends, fantasies, rebellions and confessions, will lend the full weight of its individuality.

The poetic has always existed in music, and particularly in French composers of the 17th and 18th centuries, not to mention in other countries and other more distant times. In this way, Berlioz is connected with the purest of French traditions. But he would translate that concept into symphonic music, with the abandonment and grandiloquence typical of the Romantic spirit, which was opposed to intimacy, the taste for small-scale works and the restricted world of the *lied*.

In the *Symphonie Fantastique* it is easy to find reminiscences of the French Revolution, which occurred just prior to Berlioz's childhood. Its hero, always beset by the image of the beloved, dies on the guillotine, after the brilliant march to the scaffold. But this is not enough for Berlioz; his hero will be pursued even more implacably by the furies, at a dreadful 'Witches' Sabbath' and a terrifying dance of death. It could almost be said that it is this work that contains all that the French musician would bequeath to the history of music: his paradoxical melodic inventiveness, his unique and frequently disconcerting sense of harmony, his original forms, his raptures and desolations so typical of Romanticism, and above all, that awareness of the personality of the instruments. After this, it is possible to talk in terms of a musical palette. And thus he creates the symphonic poem, which will have so much influence on Liszt and Strauss, on the Russian nationalist composers who felt so in thrall to his music, and on French musicians, even those least attracted by him.

Like all Romantic musicians, except Chopin, Berlioz felt irresistibly drawn to the two literary poles of his generation: Goethe and Shakespeare. He devotes the best of his inspiration to Faust in *The Damnation of Faust*, a work halfway between opera and cantata, and to the symphony *Romeo and Juliet*, in which orchestral impressionism can be heard for the first time. But Berlioz could not avoid the great temptation of his age: opera. Repeatedly, obstinately, he tried to succeed on the stage, producing *The Corsair*, *Beatrice and Benedict*, *Benvenuto*

Cellini and *The Trojans*, works that are now forgotten, as is the majority of his great output. The public of that time did not understand his music, and Berlioz's life was difficult and bitter, and he frequently felt disillusioned. All this was intensified by the failure of two marriages, to two women whom he loved passionately – the actress, Harriet Smithson, and the singer, Marie Recio – but with neither of whom could he find either happiness or understanding. He had to turn to activities that were secondary to his real profession. Possessed of the gift of true literary ability and great perceptiveness, he provided literary criticism in impassioned magazine articles and essays on musicography. He and Schumann are the two finest critics of the first period of Romanticism.

On several occasions Berlioz tried to enter the Conservatoire as a Professor of Composition, but without success; he only managed to obtain the post of librarian. However, in his final years, he knew himself to be the undisputed master of French music, an officer of the *Légion d'Honneur* and a member of the Institute of France. He knew of the success of his *Symphonie Fantastique* and of *The Damnation of Faust*, and was comforted by knowledge of the admiration of the young musicians of Europe. One hundred years after his death, the history of music records his name with admiration and places him in the gallery of the great innovators. The orchestra of today, with its brilliance, its expressive power and its sense of poetry and colour, owes a great deal of its potential and its greatest achievements to Hector Berlioz.

1969

Robert Schumann

Schumann belongs to that group of musicians who were born within the brief period of 1808 to 1813. The group, comprised of Schumann, Chopin, Liszt, Wagner and Mendelssohn, is the very essence of Romanticism in music.

Robert Schumann was a quiet, ardent young man, silent and impassioned, contradictory and volatile. He had sudden psychotic outbursts which intensified over the years, at first casting a shadow, but finally clouding his mental faculties completely in the last years of his life.

Schumann's studies in music started late. His father intended him for the legal profession and Robert would have struggled a great deal with Schumann senior – a good man, but irritable and difficult – if he had not died when his son was still too young to rebel. There was still his mother, but mothers are easy to persuade, and Schumann was at last able to dedicate himself to music with every fibre of his being, with the passion and excess which the Romantics devoted to everything.

So Schumann was ready to follow in the footsteps of Hummel or, especially, Weber, the composer of operas, conductor and pianist. To become a pianist, he subjected his fingers to absolute torture, to the point where he caused paralysis in one of them. Robert would never be a pianist now, nor would he ever again torment his poor, young fingers. But other torments afflict him – those of the heart. He falls in love with Clara Wieck, the daughter of his teacher, a strong, beautiful, slim young girl. In love as only those Romantics of 1830 knew how, Robert struggles and argues with his teacher – who is also his friend – but who absolutely refuses to consent to the marriage. Robert is in conflict with everything. What a marvellous decade 1830–1840 was – pure Romanticism! Over these ten years, when Schumann lives for and through the love of Clara, a successful young pianist who lives for him too, and plays his music, Schumann composes the most substantial, original and affecting piano works of his entire output. Later, in the tranquillity of the family home, with his marriage to Clara and the arrival of children – many of them – he pours forth dozens of songs; wonderful, romantic, bourgeois German *lieder*.

But, alas!, the quiet, volatile young man begins to show signs of exhaustion. Each day his silences get longer and his unhappiness more pronounced. Even so, he has to work, to compose. Schumann's activities are extraordinary: Professor of Music in Leipzig, composer, music critic and writer. It all has to be undertaken, as do Clara's concert tours, which are more and more successful.

But one day Schumann, a musician of exceptional sensitivity, hears the magical siren-song of the Rhine, and unable to resist, leaps into the waters. They only just manage to save him, but the master is now lost for good. Robert Schumann dies, after several years in a sanatorium, barely aware of the friends around him, or of his faithful Clara.

The 'Bruckner Problem'

If the work of a particular composer dulls our sensibility, shocks our taste, and perplexes our understanding, we must resort to an analysis of his music, if the composer in question comes 'recommended', as is the case with Bruckner. If this test does not calm our anxiety either, we ought to have recourse to an analysis of values that are not to do with his music, but which could be the reason for the 'recommendation'. It is what I was alluding to in an article where I referred to this as the 'Bruckner problem'.

Those circumstances extrinsic to his music could be historical, political or philosophical. Bruckner's biographers describe him as a humble man, who, without his musical ability, could well have been a benevolent, angelic monk, with a liking for sweet things. The admirable determination to present him as a gentle dove, without bitterness, to which cliché we have nothing to object, immediately makes him attractive to us.

While this gentle Anton plays the organ at the monastery of St Florian, in upland Austria, all is well. But when he comes down the Danube and is made musician to Emperor Franz Joseph, things become complicated for him and for his religious music written for the liturgy, as well as that written for the organ, which had given him a position of prestige amongst his contemporaries.

For this reason it is necessary to make clear that one is referring to the Bruckner of secular music, since the composer of religious music has extraordinary qualities. But neither should a commentator forget the Bruckner of the Symphonies and the 'sacredness' of that music, for it is wrong to separate a man into two halves.

This simple, ingenuous, Catholic musician becomes a vociferous supporter of Wagner, the leader of the party on the extreme left of Romanticism, and entrenched in a vicious civil war with those on the right, the traditional party headed by Brahms, whose musical precursor was Schumann. So we have Bruckner against Brahms. Bruckner is a rival to Brahms and frequently loses his angelic calm when he hears the jokes and slander from the opposition, or when he reads the merciless diatribes written by Brahms's friends, with their extremely sharp pens.

For its part, Vienna and its court, now deprived of its international dominion in music by the Protestant masters of northern Germany, searches anxiously to find a composer to set against the German musical invaders. Certainly, Wagner is in control in Austria and in Vienna, but opera was never as solid, pure and authentic a strength in Viennese music as was the symphony. It was necessary to protect this from the furious attacks of Brahms. Bruckner becomes the chosen one. At first sight this may seem surprising, but the organist from St Florian had qualities that were typically Austrian: innocence, clarity, sympathy for the natural world, an easy-going nature, and truculence (his well-known gluttony, which amused Franz Josef so much, is proof of this last facet). There is also a tendency to tranquil diffuseness and over-abundance, a propensity towards vague abstraction, something begun in Beethoven but quite unequivocal in that most Viennese of musicians, Schubert. We find all these characteristics in Bruckner, although in attenuated form, apart from that of excess. Because of his fervent support for Wagner, Bruckner feels more and more attracted by the grandiose, by long drawn-out structures; he, too, wants to enter the fray with a little musical philosophising, and, simple and innocent as he is, he falls into over-emphasis and unadulterated rhetoric. But what we Mediterraneans might consider to be a sin is exactly what kept the anti-Brahms flag flying: the same lengthiness and vagueness of Bruckner's music and that rhetoric, which was, in fact, able to stand up to that of Brahms. In addition, there was in this serene composer (he was tranquil for a reason) a kind of peace, of acceptance, a tranquillity of conscience, which were much less evident in the German master. In the final analysis, it was Catholic virtues versus Protestant virtues, the Viennese countryside versus the forests of the north, the impassive organ versus the impassioned piano. Proof that in Bruckner there is something that endures, perhaps even a great deal, can be found in the fact that in Mahler, also a Viennese, but of a completely different nature, there is a great deal of Bruckner. This is the reason for the love and reverence felt by the distinguished musicians who came immediately after Bruckner, who lived and learnt alongside the elderly maestro towards the end of his life. They retained their recollection of contact with that good man, a living example of those typically evolving virtues which it was important to preserve.

1950

Johannes Brahms's Symphony No. 3 in F

The majority of Brahms's great compositions were written during the summer. For Brahms it was a real joy, perhaps his greatest pleasure, to be able to spend long periods of time in the country and to give himself up to what he most loved, solitary walks for the contemplation of, and delight in, the natural world. The latter was also something that he was able to joyfully express in music, both directly and indirectly.

The Third Symphony was composed in Wiesbaden between May and October of 1883. It was first heard in Vienna that same year, played by the Vienna Philharmonic Orchestra, conducted by Hans Richter. Not long after this, Hans von Bülow, who was Brahms's most committed supporter, after the break with Wagner, premièred it in Meiningen, a ducal court, whose orchestra was made by von Bülow into one of the finest ensembles of the time. This first performance was something of a curiosity because of an event which occurred and which was rarely repeated. In his desire to proselytise, von Bülow used to repeat one or other section of a symphony. This time, carried away by his admiration and enthusiasm for this Third Symphony, he included it twice in the programme – a practice which it would be good to continue. Another curious thing about this first performance is that for the first time there appeared a group of people, a kind of clique, who 'tried in vain to spoil and diminish the great success that this symphony caused'.

Brahms himself wanted to have the first performance given in Wiesbaden – Clara Schumann in particular attended both the rehearsal and the première. She was to call the Symphony 'a countryside idyll' and in the second movement, particularly, she was sure that she could hear the prayers of the faithful beside a small chapel in the woods, the murmur of streams and the fluttering of insects. Let us note the fact that she expressed enthusiasm to her friend, in written form only, as follows: 'oh, how it pained my heart that you were so busy with rehearsals and worries, and so surrounded by friends and admirers, that you were not able to devote yourself to me!'

Brahms informed his editor of the completion of the Symphony in the following terms: 'if I find any more music from my youth, I'll send it to you as well!' From this one assumes that the first sketches for the Symphony date from his early days as a composer. For the first performance, Brahms asked for the following instrumentation: eighteen violins, six violas, five 'cellos and five double basses. 'As you will see,' said Brahms to his editor, 'this "sinfonietta" can be published in eight days'. Here is what he meant by 'sinfonietta'. He would jokingly call it a 'useless Symphony', but deep down he took the first performance and the editing of the score very seriously. The score was published first by Simrock in 1884 and, more recently, in the 1926 edition of the complete works, as opus 90.

Let us stop for a moment to consider the music of this Symphony, a few moments before listening to it, setting to one side the strange feeling (a mixture of bravery and fear) that takes hold of the conscientious commentator in those brief minutes, in which cold commentary or shallowly severe analysis is followed by hearing music from which flows an elusive poetry, created out of a serene lyricism. It is the nostalgia and innocence so characteristic of Brahms's genius.

Whatever one may say, it is undeniable that it is the musical themes that enable us to make contact with Brahms's work. In relation to this, I have said on more than one occasion that what Brahms needed in order to be a genius was the necessarily deep relationship between his musical themes and the other elements of his music. Put more clearly, the struggle, the effort of the composer to turn his themes, with their spontaneous, fluid and intuitive inspiration, into music that was well constructed and worked out, to try to encapsulate the initial inspiration in a well-conceived symphonic form, reveals that either his themes were not fit for purpose, or that he could not find a suitable treatment for them, neither in logical deduction or development, nor in the necessary instrumentation.

This terrible imbalance in composition, meaning form in the highest and most complete sense of the word, constitutes the unbreachable gap which is Brahms's tragedy and which prevented him from being considered amongst the greatest geniuses of music.

Let us try out this theory. Let us take from one of his Symphonies, for example, from the most beautiful one, the Second Symphony, a theme – the romantic second theme from the first movement. Its sweet serenity is played by the 'cellos and seems to have been inspired by Mendelssohn at his purest. Nobody with even an average understanding of compositional logic can possibly guess at what type of musical development he will hear after the exposition of this theme, which has to act as the motivating source for the development. In fact, this logical deduction or development, this fusion of theme with development, where the latter must be authentic, this balance that I have referred to already, is, in essence, what makes the music of Mozart and Beethoven endure. Unity, fusion, absolute and complete equilibrium, because this compositional logic carries both the writing of the music together with an appropriate instrumentation, all of which is inseparable from the overall achievement of the music.

This problem has given rise to the mistaken but common view that Brahms's music is tedious, overlong and meandering, when he was in essence an inspired musician, simple, clear, tender; a seductive and delightful mixture of Schubert and Schumann, from both of whom he was descended, musically.

Brahms would have achieved the perfect equilibrium or balance, to which I have referred repeatedly, if he had been able to bring about Mendelssohn's ideal. But Mendelssohn, precisely because he lacked the virtue that Brahms had, was not able to achieve this because of the lack of quality in his themes.

Would it be possible to apply this daring proposition to the Third Symphony that we are going to hear? Not in a satisfactory and conclusive way, I think. The Third Symphony may not be the most beautiful but, possibly because of this, it is the most balanced, where theme, development and lyrical expression are in the greatest equilibrium. Certainly it may seem sacrilegious – though, frankly, I do not think so – to perceive waltzes threaded through the music of this serious composer (one who wanted to be taken even more seriously), but a waltz does come to the surface during the first theme of the work. However, this soon becomes more sombre and gives rise to the second theme, another waltz, this time imbued with a sense of nature that is so poetic, so lyrical and fulfilling, that, played as it is by a clarinet, makes us see in it, as in so many others, all sorts of woodland idylls. Finally, see how brief the development is – rare in Brahms. The same emotion is revealed in the 'Andante' where, after the exposition is completed, we find the same anxiety and sadness. And so we return to the original theme.

As I have just said, Brahms was a serious composer, but his friends, admirers and critics wanted him to be even more so. The desire in all of us to be in total that which is only a part of us, even though it may be the most genuine aspect of us, is one of the tragedies of being an artist. Brahms was criticised for those lovely flourishes which enhance his Symphonies; they are original and very typical of him. They are a real delight, graceful and attractive in their lyricism and tenderness, and in Brahms's Symphonies they take the place, and formal significance, of the scherzo in Beethoven. It is perhaps because of this decision that this Symphony does not have these kinds of interludes, which are replaced by a more sentimental movement, and by musical material which Tchaikovsky himself would not have rejected. But herein lies the success of the work. The 'Allegretto' is not at all joyous and is rather over-sentimental, but its effect is undeniable – Brahms's admirers could breathe easily, as there were none of those 'lyrical' passages!

Now, after the 'Allegretto', comes what for me, at least, constitutes the best movement of the Symphony, a finale as worthy as any. Listen to how the first theme shimmers lyrically and then gives way to those sudden Hungarian-style touches that provide such flexibility in Brahms's music. Then, hear how suddenly that most desired of Brahmsian themes appears – the second theme, expressed in the strong key of C major. Hear how the themes emerge from that rich Germanic forest, alive with horn-calls. And after this magnificent movement, circular in form like the first, the Symphony comes to an end, the music quietly subsiding in an unexpected and masterly reminder of the very first theme of the work.

On the 50th Anniversary of the Death of Verdi

Without the memorial that the Ateneo of Madrid dedicated to Giuseppe Verdi, the city would have let this event go by with little more than a news agency listing. It is true that more or less the same thing has happened with the centenaries of the births of Chapí and of Bretón, whose memorials were only recorded by Radio Nacional. With no lyric theatre to speak of (it is all but forgotten), the capital of Spain is unable to offer homages of any but the most modest and improvised kind.

With regard to Verdi, there was an excellent lecture given by one of the greatest experts of Italian criticism, Domenico di Paoli, from Rome. It is unusual, but also a delightful indicator of his strong grounding as a critic, that Paoli, a member of the group which was to campaign against Italian opera (the phrase 'Italian opera' was even used pejoratively) should speak with such objectivity of the composer who did most to keep it alive. He put things clearly, with no wild claims about extreme nationalism, and no pedantic silliness about supposedly 'pure' harmonies.

Verdi was born in 1813, which means that he belonged to that extraordinary constellation of Romantic musicians – Chopin, Schumann, Mendelssohn, Berlioz, Liszt and Wagner. Verdi would have the closest links with Wagner, in terms of creating a consistent musical context. These two composers form the counterweight to the indifference, dislike, inability or reluctance that the Romantics felt for lyric theatre. Just as Wagner has been misrepresented when looked at as a symphonist (in spite of the symphonic qualities in Wagner's work, that all the world recognises), so too is it a misrepresentation and falsification of Verdi to seek to see him only as a mere musical practitioner in any form, whether it be in melodic line, like Bellini or Schubert – musicians of a previous generation, let it be noted – or in instrumentation, like Chopin or Schumann.

Verdi and Wagner were essentially composers for the theatre, in the purest and most complete sense of the word, and the theatre, on the stage and surrounded by the great construct of words, music, staging and scenery, is the context where we must judge them. We must pose for ourselves the problems that they faced, each one from his own perspective, be they aesthetic, or musical or racial. Nor should we

94

lose sight of the fact that these two men were as different and distinct from each other as one could possibly imagine two men with the same interests to be.

Verdi's musical education took a long time, though it is also true that God granted him a long life (nearly ninety years) in which to complete it. He taught himself, to a great extent, in the gods, or backstage in the opera houses. What better experience for an artist whose success was as swift as Rossini's, for example. His first works, which he took time to bring to the stage, were not the success he hoped they would be. This genius of Italian theatre could have lost his way, as a succession of incidents kept him away from all musical activity for quite some time. However, Verdi felt unavoidably attracted to the magic of the theatre, and launched himself passionately into the tumultuous game of stagecraft. The 1840s and 1850s went by; Rossini had retired from the theatre; Bellini had died; Donizetti was exhausted. Verdi correctly realised that now was his time, and in seven years he composed and premièred twelve operas and reworked two others. Nowadays, they are forgotten, but they ensured his success at the time. After this he wrote the operas that would assure his place in the theatre, and in history.

Whatever may have been the changing nuances or the ideas of the moment, Verdi's aim was always the same: to write for the theatre, in terms of the theatre, devising the music for a story, the before and after of the story, the whys and wherefores of the story, and with all the limitations and requirements, and at times distortions, too, that Italian opera high-handedly imposed on him. Verdi was always and only an Italian musician, an Italian artist and, for all the above reasons, could never have been, even for a second, anything other than a man of the Italian theatre.

1951

Giuseppe Verdi's *Requiem*

The Romantic trilogy of *Rigoletto* (1851), *La Traviata* and *Il Trovatore* (both 1853), though it has nothing in common in literary terms, offers in its music a familiar unity of melodic inspiration, and hence similar harmonies, similar orchestration, similar theatrical ideation and similar operatic formulae. After this trilogy, Verdi's fame is solidly established.

Bellini and Donizetti were already dead (in 1835 and 1848 respectively), and the voice of Rossini had been silent, for still unknown reasons, after the resounding success of *William Tell*. Now, Verdi is not only the great musician of the time, and the perpetuator of Italian opera; he is also raised to the level of composer and national hero.

Bugles declare the victory over the Austrians at Solferino, and the time for Italian unification is approaching. Verdi, who was born in occupied territory and whose birth certificate was completed in French by one of Napoleon's civil servants, participated by contributing his melodies to raise and keep alive the hopes and ideals surging throughout Lombardy and the Veneto for a great Italian fatherland.

For this reason, when the cavalry burst in, in *Il Trovatore* and the high C rings out from the tenor Manrico, as he tries to save his unfortunate mother, the audience respond in wild clamouring, shouting 'Viva Verdi', a political anagram which meant: V E R D I: Vittorio Emanuele Re d'Italia (Victor Emmanuel, King of Italy).

Verdi could not but be deeply moved by the news of Manzoni's mortal illness, Manzoni who had been hero and guide to three generations. Verdi wrote: 'I respond deeply to all that I am told of Manzoni's illness, the descriptions of his state of health have moved me to tears. Yes, to tears. Even though I am part of this base world, I still have a heart, and at times I weep.' A few days later the elderly poet, great patriot and author of *I promessi sposi*, died in Milan.

The *Requiem* comes between *Aida* and *Otello*. Verdi at the time was sixty-one years old, with another twenty-seven years still to live. He was at the height of his artistic career and with an incredible technique, if we take into account his first operas: *Oberto*, *Nabucco*, *I Lombardi*, *Hernani*, etc. The *Requiem* is similar to *Aida* in its inspiration and composition; the latter was well beyond the scope of earlier composers, although *William Tell* was moving towards it.

In a way, it would be unfair to criticise Verdi for his notion of religious music and also, therefore, for the emotions in his *Requiem*. We would then have to condemn all the religious music of a century for the way it expressed its absolute faith in God, just as it sang of love, joy and nature. By projecting inspiration through the prism of Romanticism, everything was expressed via the viewpoint of the Individual, exaggerated and excessive. This, today, seems vain and presumptuous, doesn't it? And yet, are we not simply substituting for those presumptions others that may well leave on history a less significant human impact?

Certainly, Verdi kept his distance from the norms and sentiments of what we think must inspire and sustain religious music, but it would be simplistic indeed to say that Verdi does not understand and express death like Tomás Luis de Victoria or Cristóbal de Morales – the sweet joy in renouncing much-loved things – or like Bach, or Mozart himself. Verdi sings of death in the *Requiem* like the heroes in his operas. How could it be otherwise? And the same passion and pathos that resounded throughout La Scala in Milan resonated in the same way beneath the domes of St Mark's.

In spite of our belief in musical concepts that we think are almost inexpressible, the different way in which our times consider eternity, and the different impact on our spirits caused by the idea of death, Verdi's rapture, translated into beautiful and heartrending music, will continue to move us as long as we have knowledge of, and sensitivity for, human experience.

Verdi's *Falstaff*

Falstaff constitutes an enormous advance on *Aida* and *Otello*. If these two works are almost perfect, then *Falstaff* is perfection itself. From the introduction, created on classical lines, to the rapid orchestration and voices in the comic scenes, to the truly vertiginous final fugue, there is an intense life-force moving through the score, permeating even the lesser episodes and giving them an extraordinary colour and definition. In contrast to the sense of tragedy that darkens most of the great, earlier, Verdi scores, in *Falstaff* everything is the cheerfulness of *The Merry Wives of Windsor*. No one who hears this opera will be able to forget the famous 'scherzetto' of Falstaff, the delightful quartet of women's unaccompanied voices, the whole of the marvellous third act, in the Garter Inn, with its leitmotif of the time of the meeting, the poetic idyll of Nannetta and Fenton, Falstaff's drunken scene – where the orchestra describes the effects of wine – the explanation for the strange events in the wood, the disguises and the three dances, the minuet at the betrothal… There is no doubt that the performance of *Falstaff* will be the greatest event in the memorable season of operas that is coming to an end at the Teatro Albéniz. Everything makes one hope so, as much because of the importance of the work, unknown here due to the great problems of staging it, as for the truly incomparable group, the Royal Opera from Rome, which is going to perform it.

1946

The Centenary of the Birth of Edvard Grieg

It is the case that music follows on behind the other arts, willing but slow, over the same course and with the same ups and down as them. It is a situation that is rarely contradicted. This kind of delayed, parallel development of music in relation to painting or poetry, even more so in the case of architecture, is because it is the youngest of the arts and had an uncertain and problematic infancy (though there are other causes, more complex and lengthy to explain).

As usual, music responded late to the inspiration, offered over the years, by the ballads of Schiller and Goethe, the water nymphs of Heine, the hallucinations of Hoffman, the woods, valleys, lakes once again restored to the fancy and delight of artists. Nationalist music, unthinkable before 1787, is starting to be a deliberate choice by the beginning of 1850, and a terrible divide opens up within Wagnerian Europe, which is to say, the whole of Europe. All those nations whose distinctive folklore seemed particularly appropriate for this moment hurried into the breach, happily liberated: Russia, Norway, Spain (though in our case, the situation came about in a different way, as I have written elsewhere), Hungary, etc.

How those wild, young composers unburdened their souls! For a while, one might have thought that they were going to take over the old world of music, so attractive was their exotic magic. Outdated Classicism and weary Romanticism, in the hands of Saint-Saëns and Brahms, try to make a supreme compromise, while Wagner, having definitively removed Romantic Italian opera from the theatres and taken over the intellectuals, now hypnotises the general populace.

Nationalism, an offshoot of Romanticism and in some respects very similar to it, brings to the old music values which are new, perhaps not as profound as they thought, but full of attractiveness, and fresh, youthful vigour: colouration, new notions of rhythm, various aspects of folklore, like the mystery and delight of legend, the fun of the picturesque, the free expression of ideas, spontaneity and improvisation.

There is a point in the musical history of the 19th century when, similar to what happened at the beginning of the 17th century, you might think that the laws of music, until then considered to be unchangeable, were on the point of breaking down under the assault of those young musicians who were strangers to Western art. But this art of ours was already very strong and set on solid foundations. In fact, the most secure of these foundations, those based on tonality, are precisely those on which both newcomers to the harmonisation of popular songs and the brilliant imitators of this form of song depended.

——

Grieg was born just thirty years after the last of the great Romantics, Richard Wagner, and he gained his musical awareness at the height of Wagnerism, when the struggle with Brahms was worse than ever. He was supported by Liszt, whose Hungarian rhapsodies were the fashion, and encouraged by poets, and precursors, like Carl Arnold, Friedrich Reissinger and Halfdan Kjerulf. But he always followed his own nature and temperament, his own preferences and inclinations. He had limited technical resources but was guided by a refined and infallible intuition, an instinct for harmony that was notably individual. In all, he was an inspirational musician who would come to know the delights of popularity, and its dangers. His music is marked by a bittersweet, exotic flavour, gently coloured by a discreet and delightful palette, his inspiration steeped in the popular songs of Scandinavia. Grieg was gentle, straightforward, kind and melancholy; he was the musician for the young people of his time who read Walter Scott and believed they were still living in the age of the Romantics. It is most unlikely that there would be any pianists between 1870 and 1920 who had not sighed dreamily over the effortless impact of Grieg's harmonies. They are a little mannered, looked at in the context of all his work, and for this reason, and because of his use of certain, repeated neologisms, they soon became rather hackneyed. Exalted, followed, copied by a crowd of lesser maestros, it was inevitable that Grieg was passed over, scorned and unfairly forgotten. He could even have been labelled 'affected'.

And yet, Grieg was something of a genius. Whenever we seek to know the soul of Norway, to soak ourselves in its fiords, to plunge into its mists, to enjoy the damp, shivering spring or know the deep nostalgia of autumn, we will turn to the series of *Lyric Pieces*, the songs, and the cheerful trilling of his *Piano Concerto*.

To a certain extent, Grieg is the Walter Scott of music, though he has less vigour and strength of composition. Grieg should be listened to and studied in childhood and adolescence, because he can create emotion like perhaps no other musician; he can make you glimpse distant horizons and strange nostalgias. If he is not listened to and savoured at those moments of youth, his time will never come, for it is difficult to retrace one's adolescence, and the thrill of mystery is lost for ever. The evanescence of Grieg must endure in our memories. Let us re-live it on the occasion of this centenary of his birth.

II

This brief discussion on the first centenary of the birth of the Scandinavian musician will end with some comments on his most popular work, one which broadened and strengthened his reputation throughout Europe: *Peer Gynt*.

Ibsen and Grieg, both Norwegians and contemporaries, though Grieg was considerably younger than Ibsen, were personalities that were as different from each other as two artists of the same race and time can be. However, that did not stop Grieg going to Ibsen's in the summer to offer his delicately coloured music. Nor did it stop Ibsen thinking of Grieg, when he was imagining an extended poem, almost a play, magic, symbolic, chaotic, though fused by a strange poetry of a strongly nationalist nature. The work in question was *Peer Gynt*.

The letter that Ibsen sent to the composer, from Dresden, filled Grieg with joy. In it he was asked to write incidental music for *Peer Gynt*, with Ibsen indicating, perhaps rather unnecessarily, where the music would come and what it would be like, how long it would last, even including its sources of inspiration. They had known each other for years. Involved right from his first trip to Rome, Grieg, still more or less a student, had been drawn to the already famous writer, who received him with almost disdainful courtesy and something that might have been interest, which Grieg, who was always very susceptible and suspicious of the effect that he caused in others and their opinion of him, found humiliating. This impression would never change. Grieg always felt belittled and diminished beside Ibsen. An element of technical weakness, which Grieg could scarcely admit to himself, seemed strangely to get worse when subject to Ibsen's keen gaze, for he admired Ibsen, without understanding him. This incomprehension extended also to the huge fantasy sent by the dramatist, the one exception in Ibsen's work, for it was not a play but rather a cheerful piece in its own style. Peer Gynt is a kind of vagabond, a rascal, who obeys no laws, whose salvation is Solveig's love for him, in a kind of reversal of noble sentiments.

Grieg was a musician of an essentially lyric temperament, who had to deal with an enormous work that had no unity of action or place and that wandered from the real to the surreal, from reality to legend, where the hero is one moment in Norway weeping at his mother's deathbed, and the next lying in the Arabian sun, seduced by the dance that Anitra weaves round him, or violating Ingrid, the daughter of the King of the Mountains and then fleeing for his life from the vengeance of witches and gnomes. The poor musician did not understand any of all that, neither could he understand why one would choose a fickle, perverse drunkard as a hero.

In a short time he had written the thirty-two pieces for the score of the work, which was premièred in 1876. Although it was highly successful in Norway, the play did not please in the rest of Europe. However, the music was received everywhere with enthusiasm. Precisely those qualities which prevented it being enjoyed in Europe, perhaps because they were too Norwegian, were absent from the music and were the reason for the success of the score, infused with the composer's gentle lyricism. Grieg extracted the most appropriate pieces and created two suites, of which the first would become world famous. *Morning, Åse's Death, Anitra's Dance, The Arab Princess, In the Hall of the Mountain King*, and the powerful *Solveig's Song*, which is the fourth piece of the second suite, form the first and most delightful of 'film sound tracks'.

At one time appearing on all programmes of symphonic music, this piece gradually became relegated to the modest but also agreeable position of music for the garden of a health spa, and who knows whether, in the long run, its harmonies might not have contributed as much as the waters and the freshness of the woods to the cures for rheumatics, colds, ulcers, etc.

The music of *Peer Gynt* is pure, clear, simple, uncontrived, gently coloured, like the rest of Grieg's work. It is full of unusual elements which, rather than being copied from folklore, were suggestive of it. This work, more than any other, helped establish and extend Grieg's reputation and he experienced the pleasure and the pain of being popular, of being in fashion – a fashion which a swarm of lesser musicians tried to follow, believing it was easy to copy. They achieved nothing, except to be caught up in the reeds surrounding this gentle Scandinavian siren who bewitched Europe for a while. His song will always awaken feelings and emotions in the young, which are not fully understood. When they are finally understood, they cause a pleasant intoxication that is never found again.

1943

Women in the Work of Puccini
and his *Turandot*

It would be easy to believe that this work, a favourite of the most widely differing audiences, has given rise to an abundant bibliography, and yet there are countries, like England and Spain, where almost nothing has been written on the life, work and aesthetics of Puccini.

I do not know to what extent Puccini's work has been studied from the point of view of the passionate figure that illumines it, that of the woman. If we had to reduce Puccini's aesthetics to one phrase, it would be that it is a highly sensitive gallery of musical depictions of women. In his operas, the dynamic element, let us call it, is always a woman, and the titles of almost all his dramas feature a woman.

Look at the sequence of them: Manon Lescaut, a frivolous seducer, a temptation to herself; sweet Mimi, whose life fades quietly away without her being able to speak of 'so many things' that are as profound and infinite as the sea; the jealously passionate Tosca, whose gentle hands, made to arrange roses and caress children, will knife open Scarpia's heart; some years later, the innocent Butterfly who does not hesitate to take her own life with the very sword that protects the family's honour; and still to come, *La fanciulla del West*, *Suor Angelica* and finally, his posthumous work, *Turandot*.

In all these operas, except the last (and we will come back to this interesting final work), the male roles are no more than contributory parts. Des Grieux, Rodolfo, Mario Cavaradossi and Pinkerton act within the orbit imposed on them by the strong female characters. For this reason, a slightly attenuated voice comes forth from Puccini's tenors. These somewhat passive protagonists are never, let it be noted, baritones or 'heroic tenors', as the theatre jargon has it. Puccini always returns to the lyric tenor, a voice of unusual delicacy, just right for yielding and responding to the warm caress of that previously mentioned highly sensitive gallery of musical depictions of women. They are created by one of the most sensual musicians of his time, whose harmonies and melodies alight softly upon us, giving us a sense of those warm embraces where his heroes gently rest.

Turandot is altogether different. Puccini's posthumous work gives the lie to this interpretation with which, via the weak smile of Mimi,

Tosca's tragic expression, and the trusting laugh of Butterfly, we tried to briefly characterise his work.

It is precisely in this exception that is *Turandot* that we seem to find a justification for what we have been suggesting. The pride of the haughty princess from a distant, legendary China, is no more than a shield behind which, veiled in hallowed mysteries, she will vainly try not to be overpowered. Turandot does not want to yield, because she is afraid of her own passion. For the first time we see dualism in Puccini, because the work is actually a long duet interspersed with short *romanzas* and unimportant scenes that have been seen as *verismo*. Also, for the first time, the male protagonist (written for the dramatic tenor, the most manly and masculine voice in opera) will play a part that is unyielding. He will not be a mere cipher, he will subjugate and overcome Turandot on her own ground, where she believes herself invincible. He presents himself for the cruel contest, thus humiliating her twice over.

The real nature of this exception that is *Turandot* is that Turandot is not the only one who tries to resist, though not so much as she claims, with her dubious haughtiness. What is curious, and this is the element that makes this exceptional, is the fact that Puccini himself resists, and with greater effectiveness. Otherwise, what does Liù signify? She is the opposite of Turandot. She kills herself, and all because of the kind smile of the prince, strong and magnificent, but immovable from his chosen path. 'Because one day you smiled at me' is the song. One day when the prince passed by, he absentmindedly smiled at the sweet, beautiful slave girl. Here is the authentic Puccini female character. She is the only one who knows the name of the hero, and she will accept death rather than let cruel Turandot drag out of her the prized secret, a secret which is the only way for Turandot to avoid a man's triumph over her.

In spite of these two female characters, it is not possible for Puccini to convince us, once again, that the woman is the stronger role, and that it is only because of the death of the one that the other is overcome. It just does not work. Here the subjugating, all-powerful force of the male protagonist is dual as well. His time is right and his retaliation absolute. 'Dilegua, o notte! Tramontate, stelle! Tramontate, stelle! All'alba vincerò! Vincerò! Vincerò!' ('Vanish, o night! Stars, disappear!

Stars, disappear! With the dawn, I will win! I will win! I will win!') Calaf declaims, in a resolute *romanza* written for this first 'heroic tenor', who appears nowhere else in Puccini's work.

There is insufficient space to note even in passing how this aesthetic of undoubted eroticism is expressed in music. This was our initial intention but is has been overtaken by the wish to point out another aspect of Puccini's work. It is, perhaps, the most interesting aspect, though not the only one, in the work of this favourite of international audiences.

1941

Richard Strauss's *An Alpine Symphony*

The *Alpine Symphony* was first performed in Berlin in 1915. This means that Strauss set about composing this work in his musical maturity, when he was at the height of his powers, a time of the most accomplished and magnificent demonstration of his genius. The great series of tone poems, which began with *Macbeth*, came to an end simultaneously with the fulfilment of the evolving transformation of the tone poem, which was inspired by literary sources, and whose immediate and obvious forerunners were Berlioz and Liszt.

This being the case, I would like to point out, perhaps for the first time, a curious fact, which is that the tone poem, as such, begins and ends with a symphony, or at least the intention of one: from Berlioz's *Symphonie Fantastique* (1830) to Strauss's *Alpine Symphony* (1915). There are other more profound and important topics, whose development would go beyond the scope of this review, but the fact is that Berlioz felt a kind of awe and respect for the musical forms of his forebears (Mozart and Beethoven) at the time that he was trying to create a new musical form. And the indisputable prestige of the term 'symphony' obliges Strauss to resort to it when he wishes to go beyond the general limits of the symphonic poem.

What remains of the symphony in Strauss's work? Very little, in fact. The traditional, customary division into three or four separate sections, which, though part of a whole, are independent structures, has disappeared. The *Alpine Symphony* is a single movement, and replaces what we could call symphonic structures with internal movements, brief symphonic episodes that have appropriate titles, in short, genuine musical incidents to which we will return later. This was something new, though perhaps not for Strauss himself. Certainly, Liszt had already tried to do the same, in the sonata and in the concerto, forms which have these same characteristics. But it was Strauss, inevitably, who would achieve it in the symphony. I say inevitably because what both Liszt and Strauss wrote were really symphonic poems, as I have already indicated, in spite of the names, 'sonata', 'symphony'.

In addition, something has disappeared which is fundamental in the symphony: the alternation of well-balanced themes, presented and developed on a clearly pre-set musical base, whose rules must be obeyed if one wishes to play the supreme game of symphonic creation. Thanks to these rules, we musicians are able to distinguish a symphony from a suite, a tone-poem, variations, a fantasy, etc. And finally, what has also disappeared is the very raison d'être of the symphony, that is to say, pure inspiration, music for music's sake, music that is sufficient unto itself, the unique reason for its very existence – nothing to do with intrusions of a literary or pictorial kind.

We have arrived at the heart of the *Alpine Symphony* and now its essence is revealed to us. The *Alpine Symphony* replaces all symphonic elements with a distinct programme (which is in fact more apparent than real), wide open to possibilities which are provided here by literary elements, philosophical disquisitions, or old wives' tales from other poems. At times he descends to the detail of children getting lost on a walk in the mountains, for example in 'Through thickets and undergrowth' or 'Dangerous moments', where Strauss has recourse to well-known clichés. At other times he achieves the ultimate in the expression of feelings, so that contemplation of the vastness of the landscape turns into ecstasy, with emotions inspired by musical symbols that give voice to the natural world and its spiritual essence, in ways that had rarely been achieved before.

This symbolism, coming to Strauss through his own adopted aesthetic – in itself a direct consequence of Berlioz and Liszt – is an aesthetic tendency almost as old as music itself, but which is specific to the last century. In the hands of Strauss it becomes a simple reality through his ability to garner the plasticity of Wagner's sound-world, and through his own musical nature. This caused the unjust anger of the enemies of descriptive or narrative music, and of others who campaigned for a different, opposing, style, without realising that what separated them was a simple matter of procedure, sensitivity and taste. A fair number of French and Russian composers, when looked at carefully and dispassionately, were in fact writing none other than programmatic music.

There is, and always will be, an unconscious desire – in some it is an irresistible urge – to link the music being heard to a cause, an act, a moment in time, an image, etc., far removed from the art of sound itself. This tendency, only resisted by those with the highest musical abilities, what one might call primary human instincts, has been gratified and comforted by the group led by Strauss. Their extreme skill and extraordinary boldness distracts and removes you from the straight and narrow road of pure music by involving you in complexities of enveloping mists and concepts, be they philosophical or descriptive. But it would also be unjust to deprive music of these stimuli, these developments, which in many instances have produced new branches on the tree of older musical styles.

On the other hand, why deprive the musician of the pleasure of hiding the enigmatic call of the cuckoo in the bowl of a clarinet, of imprisoning in the slim tube of a flute the merry warbling of a lark? Why deprive ourselves of the childish vanity of thinking we are 'Mighty Jupiter', making the awesome thunder crash and unleashing all the violins of the orchestra in harmless torrents? All of this, and much more, can be found in the *Alpine Symphony*. Listen to how it describes the emergence of the mists at dawn, the waterfalls, the storms, and the solitary, anguished call of a small bird before the clouds are torn asunder and the howling wind arrives. But you will also hear the majestic theme which emerges from the trombones and tubas at the beginning of the work, an imposing, monumental theme, like the mountain itself; and the sudden upward swoop of the flutes in the luminous key of E, filling our lungs with oxygen; the magical sight of perfect flocks of sheep, and, finally, the lyrical music of the summits themselves. Music, in short, which without those inspired, poetic allusions, panoramas and descriptions, would not have been created. To enjoy it to the full we need to know the sources which inspire it. For this reason, and in spite of what may be said to the contrary, we must understand the 'programme' of programme music, even if in the desire to follow it we are distracted from the very music that it is trying to illustrate. Our obedience in this way can be an advantage.

After all that has been said, what remains of the 'symphony' in this work? Nothing more nor less than its very essence: the concept of 'symphony', the ideal implicit in any symphony – controlled writing and a structured whole. When you listen carefully and study this work in detail, you feel overwhelmed by the imposing musical construct, circular in form - a real, and imagined, ascent of the Alps. It is at this point that you understand the work could not be called anything other than a 'symphony'.

Paul Dukas

Recollections of musicians I have known

In 1927, and in spite of my father's fierce opposition, I moved to Paris to complete my studies in music. My hope at the time was to study with Ravel, but he was not giving lessons then.

I was feeling rather undecided when, during those rainy days in November, they put on at the Opéra Comique a work by Paul Dukas, *Ariane et Barbe-Bleu*. I felt great enthusiasm for the composer's sparkling symphonic poem, *The Sorcerer's Apprentice*, and I made haste to go to the small, attractive theatre that I had not been to as yet. I came out absolutely thrilled, and immediately decided to work with Dukas, if he would accept me as a student.

During that time I met the Hispanist Henri Collet, and it was he who gave me a letter of introduction to Dukas, who gave classes on composition at the Conservatoire and at the École Normale de Musique.

What emotions I felt as I approached his house, in Passy, not far from the Bois de Boulogne! I remember that when I asked the concierge for Dukas, a rather short man, with a large umbrella (which he was never without) and sporting a thick beard, was coming out of the doorway, and he replied: 'That's me'. With great embarrassment I explained what I wanted as best I could, in my limited French. I thought I understood him to say that I should go upstairs with him.

An old house, a very narrow staircase, spiral as you would expect, a very simple flat, a small study and in it an old piano, some rugs, a fire that didn't give out much heat, many, many scores, and a large number of books. That's when I became aware of his French, which it took me months to understand, muffled by his beard and spoken in a dull, almost hoarse, voice. I thought I understood him to say that I should go and see him at the École Normale de Musique, and that I should bring with me some of my works. And that is what I did.

Paul Dukas was a rather distant man, not given to praise, austere, but fair in his judgements. He was sharp but not sarcastic, and yet there was something affectionate about him that came from a person who was essentially a shy man, whose ideal was the search for truth, for what was authentic.

The classroom was spacious; this time with a grand piano where the maestro was seated, surrounded by some composers whom I knew, among them Roland-Manuel and the Mexican, Manuel Ponce, with both of whom I became firm friends. There was also a small group of students, almost all of them foreign, some of whom were pianists. I happily went through the nerve-wracking audition, and months later I can say without false modesty that I was his favourite student. Thanks to his help I was able to publish a good number of my compositions, to my great surprise. I remember he said to me: 'Rodrigo, when you go to see a publisher, don't forget that they don't accept any old thing!' The following year, again with his help, I was able to have the première of my first symphonic composition, *Cinco piezas infantiles*, given by the Straram Orchestra, the most prestigious in Paris at the time.

I completed five years in his classes. After that, my wife (for whom Dukas felt great affection) and I used to sit in on his classes until 1935, the year he died from a heart attack, when he had just reached his seventieth year. I recall that weeks before he had had the first serious heart attack. When I phoned him to ask how he was, he replied, 'Don't worry, not this time!' Unfortunately, it happened the next time.

The classes, which took place twice a week and lasted two hours, were divided into two parts: the first hour was for correcting compositions; the second, which interested me more, was for analysis. At the piano, with me beside him, he would interpret symphonies, chamber works, operas, etc. His judgements were swift, assured, original, based on great knowledge, and his wisdom was far-reaching. He knew practically all music, and his opinions were always impartial. Although I once heard him say, when asked if he liked Tchaikovsky, 'I avoid listening to him!'

As a composer, he suffered from his own self-criticism. The rigorousness that was the basis of his whole life accentuated this, and led him to burn his unpublished works before he died, just as he himself was cremated while Marcel Dupré played on the organ those Bach chorales that Dukas had analysed so many times.

The Sorcerer's Apprentice and the ballet *La Péri* assure him a place amongst the foremost symphonists of our century. His orchestration is an example of how light pointillism can be sustained by firm composition. His harmonies, based on augmented fifths, sevenths and ninths, weave the richest of canvases out of an individual voice, and at a time when impressionism seemed to be everywhere. His masterpiece, the opera *Ariane et Barbe-Bleu*, is like a meeting of the ideals of a Wagner and a Debussy. The heroine, Ariane, represents his ideals as a man and as a musician: the determined, constant search for the truth, for justice, in gentleness and firmness. He proclaims this with such sobriety, such musicality, that he is a bridge stretching towards a future lyricism whose potential and influence have not yet been explored, but which could illumine the difficult road that present-day opera is travelling.

Paul Dukas, on the Centenary of his Birth

The 1st of October this year marks the centenary of the birth of Paul Dukas, a musician who was to occupy a special place in the development of the most important musicians of the second half of the 19th century. He lived and worked in France and began writing in the 1890s, by which time France had recovered from the impact of Wagnerism. His music is not easy to categorise. He is clearly independent of, but also falls between, two musical tendencies, characterised by César Franck and Claude Debussy, who battled with each other to claim the leadership of French music. But the music of Dukas would also receive the same criticisms as theirs. The respect for and knowledge of tradition that Dukas had, his admiration for his friend and colleague at the Conservatoire, Debussy, together with his own personality, comprise the various elements of his music and provide the unmistakable mark of originality in this musician.

Paul Dukas's life, until his death on 17th May 1935, was simple, modest and austere, dedicated to study, to composition, to teaching and to musical journalism. When he was still a child he enrolled in the Paris Conservatoire and when he finished his studies there he attempted to win the highly desirable *Prix de Rome*. He gained second place and never tried for it again. He worked on his own compositions and the results of this were the overture for *Polyceute* (1892) and his *Symphony in C* (1897). The influence of Brahms is evident in these two works, but a personal voice is clearly struggling to make itself heard.

Some years later, his friend Debussy produced *Prélude à l'après-midi d'un faune*, a symphonic poem which began a new era: Impressionism. Dukas became entranced by this new way of conceiving music, made from suggestion and translucence. The new thematic realm, its originality of timbre, which becomes the principal feature of this music, and its sparkling harmonic presence, establish themselves in his musical consciousness and change the direction of his work. The 18th May 1897 saw the première of what would become, together with *Ariane et Barbe-bleue*, his masterpiece, *The Sorcerer's Apprentice*. The poem by Goethe which inspired this 'scherzo', as Dukas called it, is well known. A magician's apprentice, in his master's absence, manages to make a magic broom move, and he orders it to bring water, but forgets the magic words to make the broom stop. He is on the point of drowning when his master returns and does make the tireless broom cease.

Is *The Sorcerer's Apprentice* an impressionist work? Strictly speaking, no. Certainly, it demonstrates some elements of the style: the augmented fifth, the augmented fourth, a certain distribution of orchestral instruments that creates pointillism, etc. But his composition, often fugal in form, and the structural perfection of his work – aspects which do not attract impressionist composers – distance him from that group.

In fact, just as in Debussy the new thematic concepts gave birth to original structures, so in Dukas the thematic elements, precise and clear on the one hand, and sinuous and flexible on the other, give rise to a genuine sonata form, framed by a mercurial introduction, where fragments of the principal theme are developed, and a gentle coda is included as a kind of 'moral'. Everything in this work comes from the hand of a master: its impeccable construction, its bold harmonies, and especially its orchestration, are a landmark in French music.

Two considerable works for piano, *Sonata in E flat minor* (1901) and *Variations, Interlude and Finale on a theme of Rameau* (1903), indicate another change of direction in the composer. There is no impressionistic influence from the piano, but rather, in contrast, Dukas tends here towards the style of César Franck, especially in the *Sonata*, in which we hear echoes of the great constructions of Beethoven. In the *Variations, Interlude and Finale* we encounter again the irony typical of the composer, in a work in which intellectual depth does not obscure the clarity of the musical writing. The pared-down nature of the *Variations...* allows the Rameau theme to shine through, and it explodes in sparkling clarity in the *Finale*. These two pieces were followed by Dukas's most important work, his opera *Ariane et Barbe-bleue*. Dukas's personality and his Cartesian background must have made him feel a strong attraction to this noble figure, Maeterlinck's perfect heroine, who comes to Bluebeard's sinister castle with no fear whatsoever. She is in search of truth, justice, liberty. As Ariane says, 'Above all, one must disobey. It's the only thing to do in the face of something inexplicable'. And once the women whom Bluebeard has held captive are freed, Ariane will continue on her way, searching out other truths, other injustices.

The opera is divided into three rather short acts, and their different scenes are shaped by persistently symphonic writing and a densely worked thematic structure. What we have here, undoubtedly, is the use of the Wagnerian leitmotif, though Paul Dukas never copied slavishly. In this opera he achieved a balance between the lyricism of the characters' singing and the symphonic writing for the orchestra. Dukas created in *Ariane et Barbe-bleu* a very original and expressive singing style which emphasises the serene nobility of the heroine and also provides a contrast with the orchestral outbursts in, for example, the scene where Bluebeard's treasure is discovered. All Dukas's skills combine to lend this work the most beautiful lyricism.

Finally, in 1912, Dukas produced the ballet *La Péri*, a kind of oriental fantasy, in one act with two characters. It was dedicated to the ballerina Natalia Trouhanova and premièred by her at the Châtelet Theatre. With a brilliant introductory fanfare, this is sumptuous, sparkling music, full of restrained passion. It is the summation of the art of Paul Dukas. Some other, minor pieces complete the catalogue of his work, which, though not extensive, is full of intensity.

Seen in his centenary year, the music of Paul Dukas gives an impression of complete balance: power and control, restraint and passion, originality and loyalty to tradition – these complete a personality whose principal and constant characteristic was authenticity, in both life and music.

Two other aspects define his personality: his activity as a teacher, and as a critic. As a teacher, in the classrooms of the Conservatoire and of the École Normale, he was able to educate large numbers of young musicians from all over the world, in whom he infused, above all, a love and respect for the greatest variety of music. Extremely eclectic and intensely knowledgeable – these were his norms, and those of us who went to his classes have maintained this attitude and kept faith with his aesthetic.

Dukas dedicated several years to music criticism, especially during his early years. He brought to it all his authority and keen perception. His articles on music are gathered together in one volume, which is of the greatest value, both historical and aesthetic.

1965

Maurice Ravel's Piano Concerto

The Philharmonic Society of Valencia began its season yesterday with a fine concert performed by our well-established Symphony Orchestra, featuring the admirable pianist, Leopoldo Querol, in the first performance in Valencia of Ravel's Piano Concerto. Valencia is the third city in Spain to hear this work (not the second, as is mistakenly stated in the programme), and it is a piece which demands more space than here, and publication in a professional journal, for a careful, detailed commentary. This Concerto is an exquisitely worked jewel among many jewels by Ravel. It is beautifully balanced, never tedious, and constantly surprising. The writing for piano is sharp and extremely clever. The orchestration is a marvel of judiciousness, in which each entry has been considered with the utmost care. Of the three movements of this work, I prefer the first, for its elegant playfulness, its clever inventiveness, the flow of its development, its rhythmic subtleties and pleasing originality. At times there seems to be a second theme in the form of a 'blues'. The central section is very short but is compensated for by the cadenza and the long and sprightly final coda.

The second movement is a concession to the well-known superficial return to Bach. The solo piano sings an aria-like melody which develops over a constant slow waltz rhythm, played by the left hand. This rhythm is extremely evocative, and when the cor anglais makes its nostalgic voice heard above a pianissimo background of strings and piano, faced with such serenity we forget that we are the objects of an ingenious deception.

The third movement is like a headlong race, following the sudden flight of the piano, which sets off at a cracking pace. Flutes, trumpets, bassoons and oboes rush along, keeping up with it, the entire orchestral cohort in joyous pursuit of the piano. The work ends with some carefree chords from the brass and a loud bang from the bass drum.

Clearly, this is not the gentle enchantment of *Ma mère l'oye*, nor the richness of *Daphnis et Chloë*, nor the absolute formal perfection and brilliant harmonic subtleties of *Le tombeau de Couperin*, nor the exotic fragrance of *Schéhérazade*, all masterpieces of Ravel's art. But this Concerto, in spite of its apparent concession to classical forms, obvious moments of excessive simplicity, and the clear artificiality of its conception, is even so a very attractive and enduring work.

A Ravel Festival

Those who heard the loud whistling with which certain works by Ravel were received some years ago would probably never suspect that a few years later they would also attend concerts and acclaim this musician at a festival of his works. Ravel is already a chapter in the history of music, a chapter that holds within its pages, for ever, an attractiveness that will never be lost.

For those of us who came to musical maturity after the Great War, the concert yesterday in the María Guerrero Theatre was indescribably moving. It was like seeing pass before us a film of our early, never to be relived, memories, illusions, excesses, impulses, emotions. Ravel's music is forever linked to our youth. And what a quantity of memories was awoken in us yesterday when the eminent hand of conductor Freitas Branco turned the pages of those everlastingly enchanting scores of *Ma mère l'oye*, *Rapsodie espagnole*, *Daphnis et Chloë*, *Pavane pour une infante défunte*, *Boléro* and finally the Piano Concerto for the left hand. What a homage to Spain there is in these scores, so many references to our Spanish rhythms and musical influence! We can surely feel proud. What irresistible force drew Maurice Ravel to our country, Ravel who had been born only a few kilometres from the border? This still needs to be studied.

However, there is no Spanish influence in the Piano Concerto for the left hand. In the last third of Ravel's life, another influence that would become the obsession of his final years, jazz, controls his inspiration. Ravel carries the mark of his age, that of being fashionable – and why not, for how could it be otherwise? Being fashionable was perhaps the reason for some of his music, so he could not remain impervious to the powerful and original trend in the music of his time, that of jazz. At first sight, one might think that the Concerto for the left hand is a return to his early years. That is not the case. The Concerto is in part what could be called an epilogue to Ravel's oeuvre. Perhaps realising that his life is coming to an end, Ravel allows that mask of subtle irony, which prevents many from seeing the great tenderness in his music, to reveal his emotions, and the Concerto shows us a musician allowing us to see, with great pathos, his sensitive humanity, in the phrase of inexpressible sweetness which is developed by the piano in the second section. There, all of Ravel's emotions are concentrated. But the Concerto also brings

117

us something new and unusual in the work of the French musician, an aspect that had never entered his music before – that of religious feeling. It is one of the three elements of the work, together with that of pathos, at the beginning of the work, and that of jazz, mentioned earlier. These three aspects, a 'lento' for the first two and a 'vivo' for the third, make up this one-movement work. A march forms the third, 'vivo', section, and brings together, in an inspired way, both jazz and religion – a natural combination since the two proceed from the same source: the influence of negro spirituals. All this is combined with references to the First World War. Not for nothing is this work dedicated to an Austrian, the pianist Paul Wittgenstein, who lost his right arm in the conflict; hence the musical allusions to a heroic American march, in which we can perhaps perceive Ravel's refined irony.

He still had to resolve the difficult question of a piano concerto for only one hand. Because he wanted to investigate more, the composition of the Concerto had to be put to one side so that he could try playing with only one hand. The concerto form is the ultimate compliment and gives rise to magnificent virtuosity, and nothing could be more tempting for a pianist than to play with only one hand. Ravel, however, has to devise a new pianistic style, put it to the test and find a happy resolution, which comes in an inspired and ingenious mix of 'tuttis', alternating with cadenza-like passages.

1941

Manuel de Falla

For a young Spanish musician, aware of his responsibility for his works and his words, to write about Manuel de Falla is always an act of supreme importance in his life, since it relates to his professional activities. On many occasions, thinking about the history of our music and considering the tortuous meanderings of its course, I have been strangely absorbed by the evidence of a hidden parallel between the general history of European music and our own.

I think it would be worthwhile to attempt a study of this, and who knows the possible consequences which such a study might have for our self-knowledge, and for a more exact description of the elements involved in Spanish music which bring about its originality and unusual nature. It would not be difficult to attempt, in the first place, a brief outline of this supposed parallel, starting from the nature of the different regions of the peninsula. And the reason why this has not been done, nor even suggested, as we would find in our limited and superficial contribution to musicology, would be due almost entirely to the careless abandonment by our universities of these once-flourishing studies, and from which there emerged figures capable of offering a viewpoint on the Europe of the time. Their help is essential when writing about ideas and principles related to sound. This has been, after all, the origin of so many ideas about the aesthetics of music.

Hoping that this will one day be attempted with the necessary discipline, I want to point out here the most important landmarks, since I wish to place Falla in his context with the greatest possible accuracy.

First of all, it is important to make a general and necessary exception, since we are dealing with Spanish music. When we attempt to deal with problems of a historico-musical nature, we must do so with the greatest care, since only now – and this means just a brief period of thirty years – are we beginning to have a certain degree of knowledge of this history. However, the documentation that we do have, which is considerable – not to say vast – is not sufficient, despite the finest technical knowledge, and leaves vitally important spaces, huge gaps that prevent us getting a grip on the historical scenario.

During the late Middle Ages, Spanish music – if we can call it this – borrows from others and has no life of its own. The monarchs of Castile and Aragon, as Higinio Anglés has demonstrated – and to whom we will often refer – had foreign musicians in their service, and we hardly know of any native music. Only in the 13th century, coinciding with the final expansion of Castile and Aragon, and, even more significantly, with the imperial ambitions of Alfonso X, does there develop that unique and lasting Western European homophony found in the manuscripts of the *Cantigas* of Alfonso the Wise.

The imperial ideal becomes clouded, the sense of historic destiny grows weaker, and the music of Spain falls silent. We must wait until the final years of the 15th century, the reign of the Catholic Monarchs, in fact, (Anglés asks why, and we would surely have had the answer in his book, if only he had written it) who suddenly take into their service Spanish, and only Spanish, musicians, thus beginning the 'reconquest' of the musical soul of Spain.

Everyone knows so much about the musical splendour of the 16th century that it is not necessary to dwell on it. But we do have to remember that music is the most developed of all the arts in Spain, in some ways the elder sister of them all. And when painting, poetry, theatre and sculpture continue their rise, music declines, life drains from it, and it moves rapidly towards decadence, like Spain itself.

The vitality that we find after the first quarter of the 18th century, when a joyous new life seems to emerge, is noticeable at exactly the same time in our music. And when everything is about to fall apart during the Napoleonic period, it seems that our music never even existed.

We all know about our musical renaissance, and we have to turn to this now in the person of Manuel de Falla who, for me, is its essence. We should remember that foreign critics and musicologists, intuitively, rather than with detailed knowledge, have wisely called it 'the Spanish musical renaissance.' They have spoken about the new Russian, Norwegian, Hungarian schools of music, but in the case of Spain they have used the word 'renaissance'. And it is precisely in this idea, in this truth, that we find the primary strength and the primary cause of the far-reaching power of Falla's music. Why? Precisely because Falla depends upon and draws inspiration from that 'renaissance'. It is not only the essence of his art but also, more subtly, the form, the structural constant of his art.

Leaving aside the influence of artists outside music (Roland-Manuel has drawn attention to the possible suggestiveness of the art of

Zurbarán in Falla), two masters and two environments will influence him in his early years; Andalusia and Madrid. And whoever says 'Madrid' at the beginning of the century means Chueca, his first teacher. And soon after, Pedrell. On the other hand, whoever says 'Andalusia' – in the sense of written, 'formal' music – means Albéniz in Paris; and Paris was Claude Debussy. Thus, we have built the magic circle within which Falla will have to move, and his exact geographical position we shall find in a meridian which goes through all these points, led there inexorably by all these elements: his date of birth, 1876, the Catalan-Valencian blood in his veins, the pull of Madrid, the Impressionist siren which at the time is singing its seductive song, and which takes pleasure in deceptively conjuring up the chimera of a dreamlike Spain.

For this reason Falla seems to us, judging his work as a whole, like a summary, and a summit. And therefore, in spite of his originality – and who knows if it is in this that the true strength and long-lasting nature of an artist consists – we hear so many familiar voices in his music. We follow the course of contemporary music, and in it we come face to face with one of the paradoxes of his art, of which there are so many, in that, dividing his work into strongly contrasted, distinct and even opposing periods, it nevertheless appears to us as a complete whole, one synthesis of genius.

When Falla arrives in Paris, in 1907, Spanish music and musicology are alive and well. That is to say, our art's expression and the awareness of it, have been achieved. The new voice of music in Europe – Impressionism – is also dominant. Everything is ready, then, for a musical genius to appear. We shall see how Falla takes up positions at first intuitively, impelled later consciously and intellectually by the new currents – one might say influenced by someone or, later, by an event in his life of which we are ignorant. These positions will be, first, a rejection of and a violent reaction to Madrid (the same, though less violent, on account of his character, that Turina will feel, whose life runs in parallel to Falla's until 1916). For this reason he turns to Isaac Albéniz, branded at the time by spokesmen as a 'Frenchified' musician. He will submit to the triple influence to which Albéniz's work in particular, and, in the last resort, Spanish music in general, responds – the idea of geography, the dance-forms developed therein, and the rhythms which the guitar obediently follows. These three powerful driving forces of our music, whether we like it or not, will act upon him.

And from Albéniz's influence, from that reliance on the only Spanish musician of international renown at the time, will come the four *Piezas españolas*, which appear with geographic titles: 'Andalucía', Cubana', 'Aragonesa' and 'Montañesa'. On the one hand, however, they are not dances as such, and on the other, they are not purely geographically descriptive pieces, as in Albéniz's 'Navarra', Triana' and 'Almería', but rather products of geography. And there is something more in these *Cuatro piezas españolas*, a work which is more interesting and significant than might at first appear. In them an artist of refinement has shown that he has not given himself up entirely to *Iberia*. Falla's essential and unusual quality is revealed for the first time – his reserve, that opposition to caricature, that clarity of line which is Falla's essence, in contrast with the highly decorative, even baroque explosiveness of *Iberia*. And there are other things even more difficult to express – which I have often thought about – the hesitant search, unsure still, it is true, to find a way to escape from a format, from borrowed models.

This is precisely the intuition in Falla to which I am referring. Falla understands that popular Spanish music, and in particular that of Andalusia – so different from and so opposed to the general sweetness of classical European music (if I may use this word to describe its pleasantness and clarity) – is not easily adapted to forms that come about as a result of deliberate reflection, or a highly cultivated process, both so alien to popular music. And he foresees the conflict which will break out and whose revolution is still, even today, not sufficiently clearly understood. So he abandons Albéniz, who tried to reconcile the irreconcilable, and who by the force of his genius tried to capture the *soleares* or the *malagueña* within the cold format of the 'sonata'. He abandons 'geography', and to avoid being affected by the awesomeness of what pianistic writing had become, which loomed terrifyingly over the young musicians of the time, he abandons the piano. To rise above that many-faceted obstacle, one must be a Sevillian, joyfully and happily unaware. The distinction between Seville and Granada begins to be noted. Falla now takes up another attitude of opposition, towards which the aesthetic ideas of the time are leading him – the total and intense Impressionist reaction against Classicism, as well as the one-sided one against Romanticism. But he cannot escape the tremendous pull of Spanish music, and is totally drawn to the dance – and *El amor brujo* is born.

The mature work of genius of Andalusia, the masterpiece of Falla's first period, is none other than a suite of dances. In them there is distilled the richest expression of the music of Andalusia: guitar and dance, music which is in essence the fusion of the two, achieving in my opinion the highest peak of Andalusian art.

Falla has passed through the experience of Impressionism, via the magic colours of his gardens of Spain (it is often forgotten that the true title of *Noches en los jardines de España* is 'Nocturnes'). But Falla believes then – and still believes, even though in his second period – that it is important to enjoy oneself (see Joaquín Turina's prologue to the *Enciclopedia* of 1917), and so he writes *El sombrero de tres picos* – dances once again. Yes, let us enjoy ourselves – why not? But who knows whether we may pay dearly for it! Meanwhile destiny causes Falla to produce his most delightful work, the *Siete canciones populares españolas*. We are beginning to escape from rhythm as gesture or pantomime. And at this point there will be a formidable turn of the rudder, a brusque, unexpected and disconcerting change of course. Another disquieting symptom, the *Fantasía bética*, a work condemned to wander the instrumental spheres, without any possible incarnation in any of them – and we are now in the third phase of Manuel de Falla's output, a phase which is, in fact, a preliminary one. We should have foreseen it. Falla returns to Felipe Pedrell, to Chueca: *El retablo de Maese Pedro*, and the first movement of the Harpsichord Concerto.

We can see now how Falla's output is a constant flight, an unsatisfied but fertile journey. Except that it is not a flight, in fact, but rather a constant traversing of that magic circle in which God had originally placed him. It does not matter that we do not know his *Atlántida*. It will be another line within that circle, from which he cannot escape. To be able to move away from those predestined circles, it would be necessary not to reach out for other influences, not to hesitate about his own ideas, but rather first to make a dramatic leap of faith and announce, with a flourish, how hard and difficult it has been, so that he can be discovered and admired. This is, to take an extreme case, what has happened with Stravinsky.

The place of Falla in contemporary Spanish music is clear. He is exactly at a crossroads – as was Barbieri in the 19th century – and new generations must turn to him if we wish to enter, courageously, into that labyrinth which opens before us, we young musicians who believe in him, and who see in him our infallible guide.

1977

Meeting Manuel de Falla

It must have been around 1925 when the first performance of *El retablo de Maese Pedro* took place in Valencia. That concert was a very special event in my life. I still remember, and will always remember, the intense emotion I felt on hearing that music, so fresh, so original, so much part of our history, which would point a new and broad way forward for Spanish music. The performance was given by the Orquesta Bética, that attractive ensemble founded by Falla, and which was conducted by the still very young Ernesto Hálffter. Falla spent some days in Valencia on account of this event, but nevertheless I did not meet Don Manuel on that occasion. I was held back by a well-justified timidity, something I have so often regretted, since without it I would perhaps have gone to Granada to work with him. I met him three years later, when I was far removed from all that; it was, in fact, in 1928.

We were together one morning in Paul Dukas's class when, unexpectedly, the door opened and the Director of the École Normale came in, accompanied by another gentleman. Dukas quickly got up and greeted the visitor with a warmth that was rather unusual for him; it was Manuel de Falla. After speaking animatedly to him, he called me over and introduced me. I felt a boundless enthusiasm for Don Manuel's music, and was very excited.

Some days later, Paul Dukas said to me: 'Falla wants to see you. He has something to tell you which will delight you.' Intrigued and nervous, I went to see him. He lived in a modest hotel near the Opéra Comique, beside the great boulevards, since rehearsals were beginning for *La vida breve*, *El amor brujo*, and *El retablo de Maese Pedro*. With great modesty, his characteristic trait, he told me that they were going to award him the *Légion d'Honneur*, and as a result there would be a concert of Spanish music. Herriot, the then Minister of Education, had proposed a concert of Falla's works to him, but he had refused, preferring a programme of contemporary Spanish music in which, as well as he himself, the pianist Ricardo Viñes would participate. And it was his wish that I should also take part, performing some of my works. My surprise and shock was such that I was hardly able to reply. But I accepted nevertheless.

I remember that the homage took place in the Rothschild palace, and in the programme, as well as the Harpsichord Concerto, which Falla himself played, there were works by Turina and Ernesto Hálffter. I had prepared my works thoroughly, but a dreadful fear took hold of me, and I played extremely badly; but everyone applauded a great deal. Don Manuel embraced me and said that he had liked my *Zarabanda lejana* very much and asked me to send it to him as soon as it was published. Many years later, in his concerts in Argentina, he conducted it on several occasions. The whole of Paris had been at the concert, and the outstanding figures of French music were there. I shall never forget the party which followed the celebration; it was like something out of the Thousand and One Nights! Falla did not eat anything, but as for me, my fear had given me a tremendous appetite.

The maestro used to go to a little café every day, beside the Opéra Comique. He would get there before rehearsals and after coming out of mass. He ate a very small breakfast, and used to take out of his pockets a number of small bottles full of pills, which he took very deliberately. He spoke very little, with a gentle, low and quiet voice, but everything he said was interesting and personal. He once said to me: 'Rodrigo, I am going to give you a piece of advice to follow. Don't ever sell your works to editors. One never knows. Keep a proportion of them, even a small number. I will introduce you to my editor.' Which is what he did.

Years passed, our Civil War took place, but prior to that I had applied for one of the Conde de Cartagena scholarships which the Academia de Bellas Artes used to award. I approached Falla, who was an academician elect. I have a letter in which he says: 'I have written to the Conde de Romanones (who was the Director at the time), promising him that if the Academia awards the scholarship to you, I will give my acceptance speech at the Academia.' I did get the scholarship, but Falla never wrote his speech.

When the Civil War was almost over, I wrote again to Don Manuel, this time asking him for a teaching post. He replied immediately, offering me a post as lecturer in the history of music at the university of either Seville or Granada. But I did not take up the post, as I accepted another offer from Madrid.

I did not see Don Manuel again. When he passed through Madrid in 1939 on his way to Buenos Aires, I did not know in advance; he had already left, and this time he was not to return, at least in this life. But

I had the consolation of being present, one damp morning, there in his native Cadiz, when they brought his body home on a warship, to then hear the music by Victoria which he loved so much, and to be buried in the crypt of the Cathedral to the sounds of the ocean. That ocean which had swallowed Atlantis so many centuries before, that remote Atlantis about which he sang so magically, and which was his final, almost impossible, dream.

Memories of and Thoughts on Manuel de Falla

An address by Joaquín Rodrigo on his reception
into the Académie des Beaux-Arts, Belgium

First of all I must express the happiness, the honour and – why not admit it? – the pride I feel at having been elected to this distinguished, two-hundred year old Academy, where so many great men have shone in their pursuit of art, science and letters.

At the same time I must thank my friend René Bernier for his address of welcome, and what he has said about my art and about me. I am touched by it since it comes from a friend of recent standing, and from a musician whose creativity in his art is absolute, with a refined sensibility and above all an uncomplicated originality. René Bernier does honour to both Belgian and contemporary music.

I am going to try and entertain you now by describing the career and the works of an illustrious member of this Academy, Manuel de Falla, who was elected a member in 1935. I knew him and received not only excellent advice but also kindnesses from him which I shall be happy to tell you about at the end of my talk. He was born in Cadiz in 1876, on the 23rd November to be precise. Cadiz was then as delightful a city as it is today, but its musical life was in fact very limited. Whereas folklore, *flamenco* and *cante jondo* were all the rage, classical music was only heard in a limited way. Coming from a humble bourgeois family, Falla undertook his first studies in Cadiz, and continued them in Madrid, a city which became his focus at the end of the last century, together with his brother Germán, who was studying architecture.

In contrast to the musical culture of Cadiz, that of the Spanish capital was flourishing. It enjoyed regular performances of opera, extending throughout the year. Foreign music was also to be heard. There were symphony concerts, chamber music, and recitals in which foreign artists performed. Falla chose as his guide the most representative composer of the time, Felipe Pedrell, who was born in Catalonia in 1849, and who opened the doors to Spanish nationalist music.

Felipe Pedrell, the pioneer of musicology in Spain, was at the same time an investigator of folklore, and a discoverer, as far as Spanish music of the past was concerned. He saved the music of Cabezón from oblivion, and contributed significantly to the publication of the music of Victoria. Falla broadened his knowledge of composition under Pedrell's guidance, who also introduced him to Spanish music from the 16th to the 19th centuries. Thanks to him he grew to love Spanish folklore in its different forms, and understood its qualities.

Symphonic forms were difficult for a Spanish composer of that time. The same was true of chamber music, just as problematic. There was only one means of achieving success, the *zarzuela*, whose particular popularity can be dated from the 1850s. It was a relative of the French 'opéra comique' and of the German 'Singspiel', with its mixture of song and speech. In the composer's first period, that is to say at the beginning of the century, this one-act entertainment was the form which triumphed; the only form capable of providing a composer with both income and a reputation. Manuel de Falla tried it too, but without success. He aspired to something more. 1905 was an important year in his career. The prize offered by the Academia de Bellas Artes for a Spanish opera was awarded to him. This was *La vida breve*, based on a libretto by Fernández Shaw, the first lyrical work in which we can see his definitive personality. The libretto tells the story of a gypsy girl deceived by a wealthy young man. But what gives the opera its real impact is that Falla captured in sound the suffering of the impoverished workers of that time, the blacksmiths in this case, victims of their lowly position. They sing that it is 'better to be born a hammer than an anvil'; that is to say, they are the anvils, others are the hammers. This is the basis of the opera.

Falla then feels the need to broaden his horizons and wants to move to Paris. At that time the 'Ville-Lumière' was the mecca of music. In 1907 Falla buys a return ticket to Paris for three months, but it will be a stay lasting for seven years. In Paris it is Impressionism which is dominant, in spite of its detractors. There he meets his idol, Claude Debussy, with whom he becomes friends. He also meets Paul Dukas, who will advise him and with whom he will maintain a life-long friendship. Later he also meets Ravel, Stravinsky and others.

He shows the score of *La vida breve* to Debussy and above all to Dukas, who persuades him to undertake some revisions to the orchestration. Both act as godfathers to him and introduce him to the music and theatre of the whole of Paris at that time. In 1913, thanks to their influence, he is successful in having *La vida breve* put on at the Opéra Comique, where it was performed on the 7th January 1914, conducted by the Belgian Frans Ruhlmann.

Extremely self-critical, Falla composes exceptionally slowly. The catalogue of his works is not very extensive, but his output, in which quality dominates over quantity, reveals a constant wish to evolve and diversify. He could well have cited the phrase of d'Annunzio: 'Better to die than not to develop.' Beside works such as *Cuatro piezas para piano* and *Trois Mélodies*, inspired by texts of Théophile Gautier, his catalogue boasts real successes: the *Siete canciones populares españolas* for voice and piano, which will be sung throughout the world; and the three nocturnes for piano and orchestra, *Noches en los jardines de España*, a work from his Impressionist period, sonorous, eloquently suggestive evocations, entitled 'En el Generalife', 'Danza lejana', and 'En los jardines de la sierra de Córdoba'.

The outbreak of the First World War signals the return of Falla to his own country. He manages to get *La vida breve* put on at the Teatro de la Zarzuela, the Teatro Real having refused to present the work, even though it had been officially recognised in Paris. This in no way hindered the success achieved by this music drama in two acts and four tableaux. After this, the maestro composed two more outstanding works: the ballets, *El amor brujo* and *El sombrero de tres picos*. The characters are the creations of a distinguished librettist, Martínez Sierra, an important creative talent with whom other composers as well as Falla collaborated. Originally *El amor brujo* was dedicated to the dance company of Pastora Imperio, a gypsy dancer of great quality. Because of the originality of its concept, the work was not understood at first. The public was astonished, and the critics affirmed, almost to a man, that this was not 'Spanish' music. It was only the gypsies of Pastora Imperio's company who understood that the music had been inspired by them; authentically gypsy, not Andalusian, music. *El amor brujo* presents the ghost of a dead lover of a gypsy girl, the beautiful Candelas, who is under a spell, until through the miracle of an exorcism, another lover called Carmelo, this time alive, wins her love.

After *El amor brujo* Falla composed another ballet of a different type. This was *El sombrero de tres picos*, based on a staging by the same writer as *El amor brujo*, Martínez Sierra. The story is inspired by a 19th-century novel, itself based on a traditional popular song. An old provincial governor falls in love with a beautiful miller's wife, pursuing her endlessly, which leads us to a series of varied and amusing episodes. Although it seems strange, it was a comedy theatre company, led by a famous actress of the time, Catalina Bárcena, which first performed this work. The success was such that it immediately placed Falla in the front rank of contemporary European composers.

Falla, in spite of all his success, does not feel happy in Madrid, where the artistic climate is not to his taste. The typical exuberance and wit of the *madrileño* do not go with his reserved character. He moves, therefore, to Granada, installing himself in a little house near the Alhambra, accompanied by his sister María del Carmen, whose loyal presence at his side will illumine his life. There the maestro calmly and – always slowly – composes. But above all, even though it seems strange as he is living in Andalusia, he takes leave of the music of his province, for fear of repeating himself. He also believes that essentially Andalusian music, like that of the gypsies, has brought him everything it could.

After composing *Fantasía bética*, a touching 'goodbye' to Andalusia, Falla creates a work which is surprising in its novelty, *El retablo de Maese Pedro*, taken from a chapter from the second part of *Don Quixote*. Falla, of course, does not really belong to the Generation of 1898. He is ten years younger than that group of writers who had revealed the soul of Castile, its landscapes, and its role in the history of Spain. Nevertheless, he still sets out in search of it – musically, of course – and whoever says 'Castile' means 'Don Quixote'.

The episode he chose is the one in which Maese Pedro, the old thief freed by Don Quixote when condemned to the galleys, gains his living in puppet theatres, in villages and courtyards, with performances of old Spanish legends and ancient French chronicles. Falla uses one of the chapters devoted to the Knights of the Round Table. Don Quixote appears among the onlookers, and then, to liberate Don Gaiferos and his wife Melisendra from the hands of the Moors, wields his sword to assault the puppets, even Maese Pedro himself. The work ends with a song apostrophising his love, Dulcinea, in a hymn to the glories of knight-errantry.

The score is conceived in a very special style. This is Manuel de

Falla's re-encounter with ancient Spanish musical traditions, the path shown him by Felipe Pedrell – as the latter had also previously shown Albéniz – and his rediscovery once more of the ancient melodies of Castile. To express all this, Falla decided on an orchestra reduced to essentials: oboe, cor anglais, bassoon, two horns, one trumpet, harp, harpsichord, percussion and strings. As far as voices are concerned, there are three: Don Quixote, a baritone, Maese Pedro, a tenor, and, above all, a child treble who tells the story and explains the adventures of the puppets to the audience. This chamber opera is divided into a series of small tableaux, brief scenes which the boy alone relates. As far as the puppets are concerned, they represent the action.

The musical style, in its sobriety, consists of a mixture of archaism and novelty which Spanish music had never known before, and this work opened a way for other composers to follow, among them myself. It begins with a joyful overture, as the audience take their places on the seats. Then a series of Castilian songs are heard, from central Spain, recitatives sung by the boy narrator, expressed in a half-spoken, half-sung style reminiscent of liturgical music.

Dating from 1923, *El retablo de Maese Pedro*, which contains much originality, was followed three years later by a work of a totally different character, the Concerto for harpsichord and a few instruments. This time Manuel de Falla joins hands with Domenico Scarlatti. The latter, of Italian origin, lived for thirty-seven years in Spain and died in Madrid in 1757. Falla reflects in his own language that of his classical forerunner, who had allowed himself to be seduced in the 18th century by the sounds of the guitar, the picturesque character of popular Spanish dance, but also by the enchantment of the night.

His last work, which Manuel de Falla left unfinished, was of a different nature, a kind of oratorio, or rather one of the mediaeval mysteries which were performed in squares in front of churches and cathedrals. It was inspired by a Catalan text by the poet Jacint Verdaguer, which tells the ancient legend of Atlantis. It also refers to the discovery of America by Christopher Columbus, the glory of Spanish colonisation. The maestro dedicated the last twenty years of his life to the creation of this mystical fresco, which death prevented him from finishing. He left us only the completed Prologue. This contains among other things the story which the queen of the Atlantides sings, whose music is worthy of Monteverdi, as well as an 'arietta' in which Queen Isabella praises the discovery made by the legendary sailor.

Some thematic notes and various sketches formed the basis on which Falla's pupil Ernesto Hálffter undertook the completion of the work. He turned it into an oratorio intended to be performed in front of the portals of the monastery of Poblet, in Catalonia.

In 1939 Manuel de Falla undertook a series of concerts throughout Argentina. He remained there until his death in Alta Gracia, at the end of 1946. His body was brought back to his native land on a cruiser of the Spanish navy, to be buried in the cathedral of Cadiz.

My personal relationship with this leading figure of Spanish music goes back to the period when I was attending the composition classes of Paul Dukas at the École Normale de Musique in Paris. In class one day, the director of the centre, Mangeot, told my teacher that Manuel de Falla had come to visit. He told Paul Dukas that he wished to meet me, Dukas having spoken well of me to him, and afterwards Falla always showed me the greatest consideration and affection. For example, when he received from the French government the ribbon of the *Légion d'Honneur*, a concert to mark the occasion was organised in Paris. Falla proposed that only a part of the programme should be dedicated to him, so that the remainder could be given over to unknown works by young colleagues, compatriots living in Paris. They included me, and I shall never be able to express sufficiently my gratitude at this gesture, the honour of seeing myself included in this homage given before the musical élite of France.

Following that event, I met Manuel de Falla frequently, especially on his visits to Paris, when I used to have the privilege of lunching with him. He was a person of lively intelligence and limitless kindness, reserved in appearance and quite quiet, even though Andalusians are generally talkative and expansive. He seemed immersed in his dreams, his music revealing the intensity of his inner life. By nature he was unselfish, indifferent to material things, but he was nevertheless anxious to protect the rights of composers in relation to their editors. He was one of the first to obtain from the latter a life-long percentage of royalties from their published works. Thanks to him I still benefit from this situation in my relations with important Parisian publishing houses, to whom he introduced me. In this way he showed for the first time his esteem for me, and this revealed so well his altruistic nature. Meanwhile I had met in Paris someone who was the product of a distinguished school of pianism, Victoria, who would be the perfect companion in my life.

In 1934 my wife and I were in a precarious financial situation. This led me to present an application for a scholarship awarded by the Academia de Bellas Artes in Madrid, an institution of which I have now been a member for the past twenty-eight years. At the time the Director was the Count of Romanones, a well-known politician. I sent the application to him. This scholarship was the result of a bequest created by the former academician, the Count of Cartagena. He left his entire fortune to the institution, with the aim of granting scholarships to young musicians, painters, sculptors and architects who were anxious to perfect their studies abroad. Once again I asked for help from Manuel de Falla, who had just been elected a member of the Academy. They awarded it to me immediately, thanks to his help, enabling me to leave again for France.

But the Spanish Civil War broke out in 1936. All the recipients of scholarships now had no income, since help from Madrid was withdrawn. Difficult years for my wife and myself followed once more, and at the end of our fratricidal struggle I wrote again to Falla, who had been named Director of the Instituto de España, which incorporates all the Academies in the country, telling him of our wish to return to our native land, and asking if he could help in obtaining a position for me. He did not have to be asked, and found a position as lecturer in the history of music for me in the university of either Granada or Seville, since the situation in Madrid was still difficult. 'You can choose!', he wrote to me. But I did not choose either of these, because I was appointed advisor to Radio Madrid. I also taught the history of music at the University of Madrid, a position I have only recently relinquished. These were the deeply generous actions of Manuel de Falla, indicative of the concern he gave to a pupil. Today he rests in the crypt of Cadiz Cathedral. There he continues to hear the sounds of the Atlantic, which doubtless bring him echoes of that *Atlántida* which he has bequeathed to posterity.

1978

Stravinsky's *Orpheus*

I have always felt a kind of mythic respect (never has the word 'mythic' been more appropriately used) for the legend of Orpheus, a topic beloved by the great masters of our art. They saw in it the most moving presentation of music and the glorification of its capacity to induce emotional response, as it can express the pain, no longer divine but human, that Orpheus shows when he loses his beloved wife. Stravinsky's most recent ballet, which has come to Madrid after Venice, deals with this eternal musical theme, the choice of which immediately sets before us an initial question.

Can instrumental music and, even more so, the specific music that is devised for mime or ballet, do justice to this theme? Since I do not want to commit perjury, the answer is clearly 'no'. Certainly, Orpheus represents the triumph of music, but it is a music which is exalted and made sublime by its sister, poetry. It is music made understandable by words or, if you wish, it is the triumph of words, the supreme emotional power of them when sent into flight by the moving force of music. Such a concept flows from the very choice of that myth by the first masters of opera, Monteverdi and Gluck, and all the others who saw music in terms of language. That is to say, they recognised in music only its dramatic, expressive value, by which it could enhance grief, sorrow, laughter, joy, and express them directly, unequivocally, by means of words: the art of 'declamation'.

Orpheus, with his lyre, sings, that is to say, he 'declaims', and in order to hear his song, the winds become still, the thunder ceases, wild creatures go quiet, and even the furies of Hades itself are moved by his pleas, which are intensified by language that music translates and exalts to a level inaccessible by words alone, returning to him his Eurydice, who has been snatched away by death.

Music and language are of equal importance to Orpheus, take one or the other away and he is denied his power to move listeners. The one without the other would be pointless, for Orpheus is the synthesis of both arts, and a sign of the magical power that both have when put together. A music by which Orpheus can express himself by postures and gestures and rhythmic movements suggests a false Orpheus, and such music is also bound to sound false.

The music that Stravinsky has composed for his recent ballet is short, devoid of any of the attributes or picturesqueness that might call to mind the myth. It goes straight to the central story and is made up of five episodes: Orpheus's sadness and distress when he cannot find his wife; his grief and supplication to the furies of Hades to return Euridyce to him; the brief reunion of the couple; the death of Orpheus because he disobeyed the orders of the furies; and the apotheosis of Orpheus.

Stravinsky composes all these episodes in his own style, using a language common in his work – an expressive rhythmicality, which soon becomes a formula for all those passages which lend themselves to dance: the search for Euridyce; the persecution by the Bacchantes, etc. And in a Bach-like style, for example, there are the moments of pathos, like Orpheus's plea, where oboe, cor anglais and harp achieve an orchestral colouring similar to Johann Sebastian. But, perhaps because of a lack of conviction on the part of the composer, this music seems abstruse, lacking in expressive value, the way Stravinsky wants music to sound. As such, it is incapable of giving adequate expression to the chosen theme.

1948

Stravinsky: Authenticity and Originality

The long life of Stravinsky and the rapid transformation in music over recent years mean that we have sufficient historical perspective with which to judge his work and to consider the Russian musician as one of the greatest creators in the art of music.

When his ballet *The Rite of Spring* was premièred in Paris in 1913, something intrinsic to music was definitively undermined. The diatonic mode, on which the entire edifice of sound over the past three centuries had been built, was reeling. It is well known that the first performance was one of the last and greatest scandals in musical history, to the point where some members of the public came to blows. Stravinsky was thirty-one at the time and was already very well known, due to the great success of two works, *The Firebird* and *Petrushka*. These, in spite of their great originality, continued the brilliant way forward opened up by the Russian Nationalists, but although *The Rite of Spring* maintains links with this pathway, the novelty of its harmonic chording, the harshness of its orchestration, and the provocative rhythms, disconcerted and 'provoked', in turn, the enthusiasts of the time. Cosmic powers, tribal rituals and violent, primitive struggles had been transferred to the world of music with an originality and authority that were quite unexpected. That rough, harmonic canvas, made up of polytonal games and infused with a new concept of rhythm, shook the foundations of traditional music. For thirty years after that première, Stravinsky held Western Europe in thrall, and, amazingly, each of his new compositions, over a long period, represented a new, frequently disconcerting, change of direction. I remember, because I was there, the surprise caused at the first performance of *Symphony of Psalms*. Nobody could have expected, from the composer of *Renard*, a work of such serene and profound religious feeling, of such sober beauty. And so many other examples could be given.

Music is in debt to Stravinsky for many things, above all because he nurtured in his music a rhythm that constantly enlivens it and which has increased its possibilities in a completely unexpected way. Before Stravinsky, rhythm had been the least evolved of all the elements of music.

I would like to end this brief commentary by recounting an amusing but significant and instructive anecdote about Stravinsky, which I witnessed. Paul Dukas, who died in 1935, was succeeded by Stravinsky as Professor of Composition at the École Normale de Musique where I, as a student of Dukas, had spent several years. I was extremely curious to know how those classes would be given, under the leadership of Stravinsky. And indeed, the nature of those classes had changed markedly. The place was full of young American students, intrigued by the novelty of Stravinsky's music. The composer, seated at the piano, was deciphering and playing the students' homework and they, undoubtedly thinking that it would flatter the maestro, had sulkily put together the most aggressive clusters of chords and inextricable rhythms. Patiently, Stravinsky played them as best he could until suddenly, with a bang on the piano, he shouted, 'Why, I ask you, is it necessary to write such dissonance?'

1971

Joaquín Turina

Everything has been said and everything has been written about this great Spanish musician.

Although his work is universal, the radiance of his native city, Seville, permeates it all. Seville, with its Torre del Oro, its Giralda, its cathedral, the Santa Cruz area, the tall palm trees, the cheerful bustle of its streets, its smiling, graceful women.

He was a great musician, and he was also a noble man whose soul knew neither envy nor vanity. He was a true friend to his friends. And because of that, now that we are celebrating the centenary of his birth, I want to pay this modest homage to him, full of admiration and love.

Joaquín Turina and I were good friends, in spite of the age difference, and I saw him frequently, principally on account of his position as Commissioner for Music. His office was in the Ministry of Education where I went to see him most days, in the late morning, to chat about music and thousands of other things, and to drink a glass of dry sherry which, like the good Andalusian that he was, he liked to give to his friends. He was a very pleasant man and, although he was aware of his worth, he never, ever presumed. He left us an extensive musical legacy: works for orchestra – the *Sinfonía sevillana*, for example, comes to mind; a good number of chamber music pieces, too, and many songs. He wrote a great deal for the piano. His *Danzas fantásticas*, which he later orchestrated, are very evocative, very original and very typical of him in their pianistic style, based on Andalusia, since he was a good son of Seville. Obviously, his piano music is not as complicated or as difficult as Albéniz, but it is very pleasant to play. Turina's music will last because of its pronounced individuality, which makes it immediately recognisable. It will endure, like the best of Spanish music and, importantly, pianists will always play it.

II

For the musicians of my generation it is still too soon (for me, it will always be too soon) to comment on the music of Joaquín Turina with the objectivity with which we speak of the music of Debussy, of Wagner, of Schubert, or of Brahms. Turina's most significant music is too closely linked, I might even say tied, to memories and even events in our own lives for us to be able to separate the emotional impact of the music from our own personal emotions. But one thing is already clear: the architectural perfection of his music remained faithful to an expressive imperative which, based on complete sincerity, was able to find the ideal language, form and palette suitable to communicate it. There was in the man a mixture of Christian resignation and Moorish fatalism that made him impervious to physical pain, and there was in the artist a combination of discipline and reverie. Why did people want more variety in the external forms that his music took? Did the expressive imperative that motivated it vary? It could not vary, because the discipline made possible the reverie, and the reverie gave emotion to the discipline. This balance required absolute constancy in the expressive creations of his art.

1949

Memories of Heitor Villa-Lobos

I have a great and sincere admiration for Villa-Lobos. He seems to me to be the genius of Latin America, and a musical force of nature. His technical ability is perfectly allied to his style of music, and from this special sensitivity he was able to tackle all the genres of his time.

Unfortunately, I hardly knew him. The personal experiences I have of him are few, limited to two brief encounters between 1928 and 1929. The first took place at one of Madame Molié's salons. This French lady received everybody on Mondays, if I remember correctly. All the young people would gather there, wanting to hear the latest things in the world of music, or wanting to get to know the artists who were heard there regularly, in the most magnificent way, as well as to savour tea and cakes. For a poor music student it was all a powerful and threefold temptation which was difficult to resist.

On one of those enjoyable, unforgettable Mondays, there was a Villa-Lobos recital by the Spanish pianist, Tomás Terán, in the presence of the composer. Terán was born to interpret Villa-Lobos's music. His impressive technique and fiery style lent themselves marvellously to that music, and it became more real thanks to his enthusiastic playing.

The second encounter was some time later. On that occasion, I appeared on the same programme at a meeting of the Society of Independent Music, run with intelligent discipline and a liberal attitude by Mademoiselle Boulanger. This concert was especially memorable for me, as all three of my early songs on Castilian texts were signally honoured by being sung, and repeated, by the talented young Catalan soprano, María Cid. Her crystalline voice had captivated the audience and, at the end of the concert, Villa-Lobos, who was there to hear one of his works played for the first time, was kind enough to come over to congratulate me.

We had no further chance to meet, even though our names would appear together in numerous concerts and even though we had in common both friends and great interpreters of our work. But Villa-Lobos either was not able, or did not dare, to accept the invitation from the Spanish National Orchestra, some time in the 1950s. And so I lost the happy opportunity I might have had of welcoming and celebrating him, as his personality and genius deserved.

1961

141

Federico Moreno Torroba

As our Acting President has said, all of us in the Academy feel very strongly the loss of our Director, but this sorrow is, if possible, greater for the Music Section. Together with the loss of he who was our President for so many years, there is the additional loss of one who was a friend, as well as one of the most significant musicians of our time.

As we all know, Federico Moreno Torroba was a distinguished representative of what is undoubtedly the greatest period of our *zarzuela*. He and Pablo Sorozábal were able to bring to fruition, after long development, our most characteristic lyric art form. His work, like his life, was one of incessant and developing activity. Not long ago, I heard him say that he had already written more than a hundred works, more than a hundred *zarzuelas*. If we take into account that each one has two or more acts, it comes to an incredible amount of music. And it was music that was always well written, always inspired, always linked to the best traditions of this genre.

Indeed, if we wanted to find his musical predecessor, we would have to go back to the end of the previous century, to Fernández Caballero, the composer of *La viejecita, Gigantes y cabezudos*, and *Las dos princesitas*. Like him, Moreno Torroba wrote music of easy inspiration, of great melodic elegance. They were melodies of his time, never clichéd, but always within the *zarzuela* tradition, always closely linked to the dramatic requirements and to the particular psychology of the characters. He also had a very sure sense of harmony, which was never 'vague', and an orchestral sound that was unusual in the realm of the *zarzuela*. In this context, I would mention the work that is undoubtedly his masterpiece, and one of the best *zarzuelas* of this century, *Luisa Fernanda*. There is also *La marchenera, La Caramba*, or his last *zarzuela*, *Baile en Capitanía*. At a difficult time for popular Spanish lyricism, after the likes of Serrano Vives, and Pablo Luna, Moreno Torroba was able to maintain the quality and continue it with his hundred or more musical scores, which compare very favourably with those of his more illustrious predecessors.

Moreno Torroba not only composed *zarzuelas*; he also wrote a one-act opera, *La virgen de mayo*, a work of his youth, premièred at the Teatro Real, and at the end of his life he added the three-act opera *El poeta*, a work which we applauded with real enjoyment two years ago. This opera not only represents the very best of his theatrical works, it is also unique in the history of music, as no other composer has written an opera at 88 or 89 years of age!

To this remarkable output we should add another interesting area of musical activity, his instrumental compositions. Here we find a large group of pieces written for guitar. Incidentally, Moreno Torroba was one of the first modern composers to turn his attention to this instrument, led to it by its beauty and by the encouragement of his great friend, Andrés Segovia, who was to do so much to create a special repertoire for the guitar. Moreno Torroba wrote many works for the instrument but it is sufficient to name his *Sonatina*, written in the twenties, and which should figure in the repertoire of all guitarists. As well as impeccable writing (which we all know is not easy), Moreno Torroba's guitar compositions show a level of excellence in his harmonic style and an extensive range of themes, constantly renewed, while remaining within the best guitaristic style. His style and technique are at their finest in the various Concertos, for guitar, and for four guitars and orchestra. He also left some works for other instruments, and on the 30th May last our friend Ramón Amezúa, with his usual mastery, introduced us to three preludes in the best organ style. Additionally, in the current season, we will hear Moreno Torroba's posthumous creation: a concerto for piano and orchestra which, together with various ballet scores, round off his work.

I must add two further things to all this admirable activity: first, that of promoter of the *zarzuela* genre to which he more or less dedicated the whole of his life, on many occasions not only for himself but to make known the works of numerous colleagues. He often expended his private wealth on this risky business, since his campaigns were typified by the greatest detail and careful selection in the staging of new works or those of the better-known repertoire.

The second activity in his very busy life was carried out at the head of the Sociedad de Autores de España, first as Vice-President and then, in recent years, as President. During his presidency a very hard task awaited him, and he had to work assiduously to correct the defects, not to say vices, of the organisation – a difficult job in something as delicate and complex as are the head office and administration of a Society with a thousand branches overseas, which handles hundreds of millions of pesetas. He travelled frequently and widely, sometimes to conduct his own works, sometimes to attend meetings at international gatherings. He was always accompanied by his daughter, Mariana, who was also his friend and secretary, whose charming, *madrileño* wit was able to distract him from those serious problems which robbed him of many hours during his long life, and which have undoubtedly deprived us of a good number of works.

Now we are left with his imperishable memory and recollections of his charm, his agreeable companionship. Above all, we are left with his example, an example that is simply legendary.

1982

Frederic Mompou

The phrase that best defines Frederic Mompou is that he was the Spanish 'poet of the piano'. He was also the best interpreter of his own work. It was always a delight to listen to him, because he played like nobody else. He wrote memorable pieces, both for piano and voice. And, personally, he was a great artist, a gentleman. A man of refinement.

I liked him tremendously... we liked each other a great deal. Recently, however, we were not in contact much, but when I went to Barcelona or he came to Madrid, we saw each other whenever we could. More than anything else, I recall his kindness, his distinction, the clarity of his judgements, the poetry of his music. It was very Mediterranean and, in spite of being at times full of French Impressionism, was always totally Catalan.

1987

Luigi Dallapiccola

Last year, Dallapicola visited several Spanish cities, especially Madrid and Barcelona, accompanied by Gaspar Cassadó. Such access to music, facilitated by the composer himself, is highly desirable, and it is to be hoped that music will become better known and familiar to the public by direct contact with composers, who are somewhat distant from their listeners.

Dallapicola is undoubtedly the one who generates most interest amongst the Italian composers of his generation – a generation who could be called young maestros, for Dallapicola is just touching fifty years of age. An intense Florentine, seduced by everything that requires exploration and experience, he has engaged with dodecaphonism and is the best-qualified representative of this style in Italy, a style that has been very popular amongst those young people. His output is not very large. Though this article does not intend to be exhaustive in any way, it does refer to the most important works: a short concerto for piano, which he performed himself; two short operas, *Volo di Notte* and *Il prigionero*; a few works for solo instruments or small ensembles; his composition titled *Tartiniana*, for violin and orchestra, which we know of thanks to Josefina Salvador; and the *Variazioni* for orchestra, one of his most recent compositions. Finally, his best-known work, which has assured his reputation, *Canti di Prigionia* for choir, two pianos, harp and various percussion instruments. The choir of Radio Nacional, with their conductor Odón Alonso, gave the first performance of this work, in the presence of the composer, and to great acclaim.

Setting aside the two operas mentioned above, which are not known in Spain, the remainder of his work listed here sets before us a composer overtaken by anguish – that much-vaunted anguish into which our times seem to have sunk. Yes, his music is anguished, but it is never harsh. It throbs with the effort to render dodecaphonism into sincere expression. It seeks to eliminate all that could appear facile or shallow. What may be mathematical in this style of music becomes (or tries to become) in his hands emotion that is sincere, I would even say 'pleasant', if the word weren't so discredited. Here lies the paradox: that anguish can be 'pleasant' for us. This is the power of Dallapicola's art, of his efforts with what I called earlier the elimination of the mathematical – of his desire, frequently achieved, to provide us with music, real music.

For me, and I think for everybody, his masterpiece up to the present is the *Canti di Prigionia*, a work of unexpected difficulty for choirs but which, once the difficulties are overcome, leaves only the deep emotion of its message. From three Latin texts about historical figures he constructs three movements which comprise one of the most original works of our time. The rainbow colours of the orchestra contrasting with the sustained notes of the choir form a unity of colour and emotions that only Italian dodecaphonism, so much less harsh and profuse than that of Germany, could produce. Here Dallapicola achieves what for me is the ideal in any system: a new form to express a new art. And this is the struggle that Dallapicola pursues – sometimes he wins and sometimes he does not. Behind him comes a generation of young Italians who follow his lead in the efforts I mentioned previously, and some examples of whose work I heard not long ago in Baden-Baden.

1956

Alfonso Letelier and Music in Chile

For some months now one of the most attractive figures of the young South American music scene has been living here, Alfonso Letelier. I have had the good fortune to spend some time with him and his distinguished wife, an excellent artist in her own right, though the time has seemed short, so interesting is his personality and the things he has told us about how they have been able to create a School of Music in Chile. There is so much from which to select examples and ideas. In this article I cannot include as much as I would like, but at least it would be good to give an idea here of our conversations, when two musicians got to know and to appreciate each other:

My dear Letelier, forgive me, but please tell me how old you are.

With great pleasure! I was born in Santiago, Chile, in 1912. I don't know if this will surprise you, but I did my studies in music at the Conservatoire of the University of Chile, at the same time as I was studying engineering.

A wonderful combination! And perhaps that's why one can see in your music a perfectly achieved ideal of form. In this respect, I've been impressed by your Sonetos, *by Mistral, for soloist and orchestra. They remind me a little, in their depth and their kind of quiet pathos, if I can use the phrase, of Mahler's* Das Lied von der Erde.

Exactly, and though it may surprise you, in Chile we are aware of the latest and most significant developments in Europe. Since 1925 the music scene in Chile has been very dynamic. The initiation and realisation of it all is due primarily to Domingo Santa Cruz, with the creation of the Bach Association. They set up courses in music there and brought about the reform of the Conservatoire and the establishment of the Symphony Orchestra and the Faculty of Fine Arts. The orchestra is led by Armando Carvajal, a musician of extraordinary ability as a conductor. Weekly concerts are given all year round in which the audience hears the best of the world's music, both classical and modern.

This is an audience which was hesitant to begin with, snobbish soon after, but finally, cultured and genuinely enthusiastic.

Within a short time, Santa Cruz obtained official approval to create the Institute of Advanced Music, for which the State Orchestra and the School of Dance were also set up, and soon a School of Opera will be created. We don't neglect the work of spreading culture. Every Sunday there are concerts for workers, with commentaries on the works performed. They have had marvellous results.

The Institute pays attention to the most subtle and refined areas of music, with numerous concerts of chamber music. And all of this is extended into the provinces, with tours by the State Orchestra. In all these concerts they expect Chilean music to be played, if possible. We did have problems at the beginning, but our audiences have eventually become interested in Chilean works, because it's their own music. Armando Carvajal is really committed; for example, he'll make every effort and sacrifice to enable us Chilean musicians to hear our compositions, and in this respect we can't thank him enough for what he does for our music. Because of it, we have today a genuine symphonic repertoire.

Yes, I've been aware of this through your works, and those that you've played to me by Santa Cruz, Allende and others. It's work that is proof already of considerable maturity, that seems well supported and popular. But don't try and fob me off – I want to hear more about your own work!

There is little of interest, if we compare it with what I've just been telling you about. In 1935 I met my wife's family and we soon put together a vocal quartet, with Margarita, Blanca y Gabriel Valdés. We sing everything interesting, both classical and modern, but we've also gone further. I also conduct a huge choir of over four hundred voices that has performed all the polyphonic works.

I see that, in spite of your youth, your output is already very extensive.

I don't know – I try to work as much as I can. I have written a *Suite burlesca*, whose poems you have so kindly referred to; *Balada* and *Canción*; a quite substantial number of songs, both for choir and for solo voice; and in recent years, I have composed *Cuatro canciones*, the *Vida del campo*, a string quartet, etc.

And what next?

Now, I'm going home, delighted by your country's hospitality, and there I will try to make known the music of Spain, which is so fresh, rich and exciting. You do not make enough of your own music – and that won't do nowadays!

I say goodbye to Alfonso Letelier and Margarita with sadness. This last conversation, like so many others, has brought me knowledge of music and names that I scarcely knew. Spain needs quickly to get to know the music of Adolfo Allende, founder of the School, of Santa Cruz, Letelier, Enrique Soto, Iramit, Catepos, Bisquert, Leng, Negrete, María Luisa Sepúlveda, Juan Casanova, René Amengual – names which today are familiar to me because of the glowing tributes from this great artist. He too knows our composers and admires our music, as well as the performances of the Orquesta Nacional, one of the best he has heard – those are his own words.

And so, saying farewell to Margarita and Alfonso Letelier, let us hope that there will be reciprocal knowledge of the music of both our countries. Nothing would give me more pleasure, nor be more easy and beneficial to us all. We must not forget that music, uniquely among the arts, can bring nations together.

1947

SOCIEDAD FILARMÓNICA D VALENCIA

CURSO XVI   1926-1927

CONCIERTO XIV

232 DE LA SOCIEDAD
16 DE FEBRERO DE 1927

ORQUESTA SINFONICA

DE VALENCIA

DIRIGIDA POR EL MAESTRO

J. MANUEL IZQUIERDO

TEATRO PRINCIPAL   A LAS 6 DE LA TARDE

Valencia concert poster 1927.

The Paul Dukas class 1928.

Ecole Normale de Musique de Paris

— 114 bis, BOULEVARD MALESHERBES —

DIMANCHE 6 MAI 1928, à 3 Heures

Premières Auditions d'Œuvres des Elèves de la Classe de Composition
DE M.

PAUL DUKAS

PROGRAMME

1. **Deux Pièces pour piano** .. .. Tudor CIORTEA
   a) Musique croisée
   b) Romance pour toujours
   M DRIMBA

2. **Suite roumaine** pour piano. Romeo ALESSANDRESCO
   M. DEMETRIADE

3. **Doïna** .. .. Tudor CIORTEA
   Mlle SAFTU

   Gracieuse est la Demoiselle .. .. Joaquin RODRIGO
   La Nuit (N. Lilieff) . .. . Lubo PIPKOFF
   Iberia (Pierre Reyniel) .. .. José ROLON
   Mlle Denise PARAF

4. **Deux Pièces pour piano** .. .. Lubo PIPKOFF
   L'AUTEUR

5. **Miniatures**, pour quatuor à cordes .. Manuel PONCE
   **MM. VOULFMAN, FIGUEROA
   BLANPAIN, RECULARD**

6. **Consentement** (Pierre Reyniel) .. .. .. José ROLON
   Cloches »
   Mme Clema de PONCE

7. **Sarabande lointaine**, pour instruments
   à cordes . .. . Joaquin RODRIGO
   **Double quatuor sous la direction
   de M. D. ALEXANIAN**

   PIANO PLEYEL

INVITATION POUR DEUX PERSONNES

IMP. G. LABACHE & CO.—NANTERRE

École Normale concert poster 1928.

THÉATRE DES CHAMPS-ÉLYSÉES, 13, avenue Montaigne

16 CONCERTS D'ORCHESTRE

SOUS LA DIRECTION DE

WALTHER STRARAM

SAISON 1929

Tous les Jeudis soir

DIXIÈME CONCERT

JEUDI 28 MARS, à 9 heures du soir

PROGRAMME

L. van BEETHOVEN . . . Symphonie n° 8.

J. IBERT . . . . Escales.

J. RODRIGO. . . . . Cinq pièces enfantines

1ʳᵉ audition

C. DEBUSSY . . . . . La Mer.

Prix des Places : de **2** *francs à* **40** *francs*

Le Concert commencera strictement à l'heure indiquée.

Location { THÉATRE DES CHAMPS-ÉLYSÉES, 13, av. Montaigne.
{ Maison DURAND, 4, place de la Madeleine.

Abonnement : au THEATRE DES CHAMPS-ÉLYSÉES.

11ᵐᵉ Concert : le Jeudi 11 Avril 1929.

Straram concert poster 1929.

154

Joaquín Rodrigo in Salzburg 1935.

Joaquín Rodrigo the writer.

Curso para Extranjeros

La música instrumental en las Cortes Imperiales de España

Tres Conciertos-Conferencias

por el

Maestro JOAQUIN RODRIGO

Compositor y Profesor de Historia de la Música

Con la colaboración de la cantante

JOSEFINA RODA DE ARAMBARRI

Ateneo de Santander

21, 23 y 24 de Julio, a las siete y media de la tarde

1938-III AÑO TRIUNFAL

INVITACIÓN

Curso para Extranjeros Santander 1938.

A Braille page from the Concierto de Aranjuez *1940.*

The same page as printed music.

Concert poster for the première of the Concierto de Aranjuez *1940.*

Joaquín Rodrigo in the late 1940s.

Real Academia de Bellas Artes 1951.

Lecturing at the University in the 1950s.

With colleagues from the Real Academia de Bellas Artes 1979.

The Vaqueroturcios portrait 1986.

Joaquín and Victoria Rodrigo 1986.

Joaquín Rodrigo at the Palace of Aranjuez 1992.

Rodrigo on his own Music

Rodrigo on his own Music

Faith

For me the greatest virtue of an artist is not related directly to the art he practises, in this case music, but is inherent in all the arts, as it is in morality and philosophy. This virtue is faith. I believe that without faith in the art which is cultivated, and without faith in oneself, our artistic images will be false and will therefore lack character, which is what in the final analysis has a permanent value. Faith, of course, borders on presumption, as does thrift with miserliness, but to combat that danger we have an antidote in modesty.

I believe it is necessary to be satisfied when one composes, at least at the time, in order to be able to create a work that will last. These are the moments of faith to which I have referred. Melodic inspiration, striking harmonies, rhythmic invention, and formal perfection, are secondary agents; their values vary in different ages because of different aesthetic perceptions. The important thing is the permanent power of inspiration. And for me this is none other than faith.

The Guitar, Inspiration of Spanish Music

I have said elsewhere that if we wished to put into a formula the essence of Spanish music, this formula would be written with just two words, 'geography' and 'dance'. Geography and dance, or what is in this case the same thing, landscape and rhythm, give rise to eighty per cent of our music, and we composers of Spain find in them the primary, most entire and original motive of our inspiration. Leaving aside for now the influence of the medium itself, that is to say the possible transmutation into art of the sounds of one particular geographical location, or the evocation of a city by the action of this same art (something which would open before us an astonishing map of sonorities), let us for a moment fix our attention on the second of the constituent elements of our music, on the second word of the formula chosen to exemplify Spanish music: the dance.

To say 'dance' is to say 'rhythm'; and rhythm in Spanish terms means 'guitar'. But what precisely is this guitar? What kind of instrument is it that the composers of Spain hear in their moments of greatest intensity? It is – as I have said before – a strange instrument, gigantic, multiform and fantastic, an instrument which has the tail of a piano, the wings of a harp, and the soul, in fact, of a guitar. This phantom, this impossible sonority, created by the imagination of the Spanish musician, is what inspires our music. One hears within it a strange and rare piano which in the last resort is not a piano, and an original and unique orchestra, which is not an orchestra either; but it is this orchestra and piano which show the measure of our originality. One can find in our music – and everywhere – mediocre works written for piano, even by the greatest masters; but not written for the guitar. This fact has given me cause for thought not a few times, and in it I find confirmed the theory I have expounded for many years. 'An expressive spinet', Debussy called it. 'An instrument which is heard little, but which makes its mark', said Stravinsky.

The guitar, inseparable companion in the 16th century of pedlars and tramps, travelling barbers and pícaros, who scratched the scabs on their hands with their strummings. That simple instrument, harsh and primitive, companion of carters and nomads, which enjoyed spending the starlit nights in the corrals of inns, or palace attics, playing *jácaras* or *seguidillas*…, at times approached the doors of grand rooms on tiptoe, and stayed there as though transfixed and dumbstruck, listening to its fortunate aristocratic sister, the vihuela, played by the skilled, refined hands of the musician and courtier, Luis de Milán. There was in the lowly instrument's unwonted flight almost an intuition of its lofty destiny. It was like a shadowy recognition of what was foretold. Not many years were to pass before the first guitar manual was published, in 1586, by that good and famous Catalan doctor, Juan Carlos Amat, 'doctor, and musician when God deigns to improve my lot', he said of himself. And very soon the guitar goes from four to five strings, and from five to six; and it is not long – imagine! – before it supplants the proud vihuela, which dies out at the close of the same century, victim of its own complexity and greatness, and of the 17th century passion for the theatre. Room will be found in the latter for the guitar, the guitar which does not mind accompanying the brazen dances of the players. And not long after, brought by other hands, courtly and musical, it arrives in the chamber of King Philip IV.

From Gaspar Sanz to Sor it is but a step; and but one more from Sor to Tárrega. This mere yesterday opens its gates to the joyful present day, the splendid and mature reality of the most Spanish of all instruments.

Concierto de Aranjuez

*Joaquín Rodrigo wrote and spoke in interviews many times about his
most famous work, following the première of the Concierto de Aranjuez in
1940. He understandably repeated several of his ideas on different occasions,
and the following is a synthesis of what he wrote and said over the years.
The notably imaginative and poetic language employed in places was
a constant feature of these commentaries.*

I

Many years have passed since I composed this work, in the Latin
Quarter in Paris, as I was waiting to return to Spain. Today, thanks to its
music, to its performers, and to the flag which the historic and poetical
name of 'Aranjuez' suggests, the Concerto, enclosed within the body of
the Spanish guitar, now travels the entire world.

The *Concierto de Aranjuez* was written in Paris in the winter and
spring of 1939 and was completed a short time afterwards in Madrid. It
was premièred on the 9th November the following year, with a success
unprecedented in Spanish music. The performers then were Regino
Sainz de la Maza and the Barcelona Philharmonic Orchestra, conducted
by César Mendoza Lasalle. The most responsible critics greeted the
work with the greatest acclaim, and were united in pointing to the
date of its première as an historic moment in the country's music. 'In
fact', wrote one music critic, 'it is not possible to find in Spanish music
another work which presents more picturesque suggestiveness, or
greater formal perfection. For the first time in the history of our music,
a combination of picturesqueness and Classicism balance and enliven
each other.'

The *Concierto de Aranjuez* takes its title from the famous royal
residence fifty kilometres from Madrid, on the road to Andalusia, a
place particularly favoured by the Bourbons. Although this Concerto is
a piece of pure music, without any specific programme, its composer, by
identifying a specific place – Aranjuez – intended to indicate a particular
time – the end of the 18th and beginning of the 19th centuries, the
courts of Charles IV and Ferdinand VII, a subtly stylised atmosphere of
majas and bullfighters, and of Spanish sounds returning from America.

The guitar, with notable daring, is pitted against the whole orchestra, which comprises piccolo, flute, oboe, cor anglais, two clarinets, two bassoons, two horns, two trumpets and strings. The guitar is the soloist throughout, but the orchestra is a real delight, transparent, shining and constantly sparkling.

The first movement ('Allegro con spirito') is animated throughout by the same joyful rhythmic impulse, with its two constituent themes never interrupting the headlong progress of the music. The second ('Adagio') presents an elegiac dialogue between the guitar and the solo instruments of the orchestra – cor anglais, bassoon, oboe, horn, etc. – and an uninterrupted pulse, four beats to the bar, supports the whole sonorous edifice. The third movement ('Allegro gentile') evokes a courtly dance, in which the combination of two- and three-beat bars, as well as the lightest scoring, keeps the rhythm alert throughout, until the final swift *fermata*.

II

Throughout Spanish music there circulates, diluted in its veins and communicating to it its deep heartbeat, the unusual influence of a strange instrument, at once fantastic, gigantic and multiform, which is idealised in the ardent imaginations of Albéniz, Granados, Falla and Turina. It is an instrument which has the wings of a harp, the tail of a piano, and the soul of a guitar. This soul is crystallised for the first time in the *Homenaje a Debussy* by our great master, Manuel de Falla. And so the guitar has now left the hands of ordinary players, but is imbued with popular styles, and its technique has been extended prodigiously, thanks to the extraordinarily sensitive and delicate fingers of Tárrega. This Spanish instrument, in the hands of a famous group of guitarists, traverses the entire world, receiving the fervent homage of the greatest composers, who enrich its repertoire with new compositions. Stravinsky even uses the guitar as an ensemble instrument.

Once the concept for my Concerto was formed, it became important to situate it in an era, and, even more, in a particular place – a time during which the *fandango* had been broken up into *fandanguillos*, and *cante hondo* and *bulerías* shook the Hispanic world – Charles IV, Ferdinand VII, Isabel II, Aranjuez, America…

It was not sufficient for great virtuosos to shine as soloists; they also needed to stand out amidst and above the instrumental accompaniment, with supreme displays of their technique. The concerto was born from this desire, a sumptuous and decorative form, which, by dint of confronting an instrument with an orchestra, considerably expanded the capacity of solo instruments. The same step was required of the guitar, and this sudden development created a series of unexpected technical problems, which Sainz de la Maza has not only had to resolve but also to conquer.

It would be wrong to expect power in this Concerto of mine, and one can look in vain for great sonority; that would be to falsify the guitar's essential nature, and debase an instrument which is capable of creating the subtlest of sounds. Its strength is to be found in delicacy, and in intense contrasts. The music of the *Concierto de Aranjuez*, a synthesis of the classical and the popular, of form and feeling, sounds forth – hidden in the breeze which moves the leaves of the gardens – and only wishes to be strong like a butterfly, but as tightly controlled as a *verónica*, the pass of a bullfighter's cape.

III

It is far from being my intention to attempt here a criticism of my own Concerto, given its first performances in 1940 in quick succession in Barcelona, Bilbao and Madrid. Self-criticism is an uncertain terrain, especially in our country. But I would like to indicate certain intentions of mine, and the reason for a number of apparent aims which, to the refined taste of intelligent connoisseurs, might perhaps appear to be in conflict.

Thinking of a guitar concerto, after Sainz de la Maza and the Marqués de Bolarque induced me to write it, two problems clearly stood out among many. In the first place it was necessary to achieve a clearly defined orchestration, sufficiently strong to give weight to the ephemeral sound of the guitar, and at the same time to be so light as to not drown the subtle sounds of this Spanish instrument, except for those occasions when the orchestra covers any instrument, including even the piano. I could not do what one does in similar circumstances, study previous examples. I did not even know the quintets which Boccherini wrote for the guitar, and which can be considered the outstanding attempt to blend this solo instrument with the string quartet. Lacking musical examples, therefore, it was necessary to resort to literature.

In answer to a question, Debussy once wrote that 'the guitar is an expressive spinet', and I think this is the best thing that has ever been said about this instrument of ours. This phrase was the starting point and also the promise of what might be accomplished in the concerto which Regino so desired. From 'expressive spinet', which is the guitar, we can go back to the harpsichord, essentially a plucked organ, and from that to what constituted the orchestra in much earlier times, the 17th-century organ itself. There is a predominance of reeds, very light harmonic foundations, and, most importantly, an intensity of expression, proceeding via clear contrary positions and strong contrasts, which are created from a number of different keyboard styles. In theory at least, the first and most difficult question was resolved, and its resolution opened the way to the second – the kind of concerto it was appropriate to write.

Our guitar is the only survivor of the rich and highly varied instrumental life-forms of the Middle Ages. In the depths of its harmonic possibilities, the soul of the Moorish guitar – 'harsh notes and piercing voices' – attempts to combine, not without a struggle, with that other soul, of another Latin 'guitar' – the lute, from whose rounded form delicate plucked notes were to be heard. There was Gaspar Sanz's guitar, too, influenced by Calderón's, in the decadent court of the last Hapsburg monarchs; and the strummings of common people; the noble sounds of the courtly vihuela of Luis Milán; sensualities from across the seas, caught in the masts of immigrants' guitars; and a court that was alive to all this… Aranjuez! From a *bulería* to a distant *pasapié*. It is good for fantasy to be released – reality comes later. The struggle with difficult material is often impossible, and one is satisfied if just one of these fantasies comes to life.

Sainz de la Maza's art has achieved all this in the face of a hard but deliberate struggle. He has made the guitar sound as Stravinsky said it sounded – penetrating yet distant – and what a pleasure it was for me to see all my anxieties more than satisfied by three very different audiences. The fearlessness of two young conductors, with fewer doubts than the composer himself, contributed to this success: César

Mendoza Lasalle, the first to believe in the work, who premièred it in Barcelona, and whom we thank for his warmth and encouragement; and Jesús Arámbarri, a devoted colleague, full of enthusiasm, who conducted it in Bilbao and Madrid.

IV

On more than one occasion I have said that criticism of one's own music, applied to this or that work, in a country like ours, of undoubted mistrustfulness and malice, seems to me rather futile, or even dangerous, if it is done seriously. The composer, therefore, in order not to appear vain, has to slide humbly over what he believes to be his clear successes, the things he has achieved, and rail against, even show anger, at what he believes and judges to be his errors; in professional slang, his 'blunders'. If he did not do this, it would produce in the reader, or in this case, the listener, the following monologue: 'Good Lord, what a way to flatter oneself! That's hardly justified!' Or perhaps: 'Ah, just as I thought, that passage doesn't sound too good, and when the composer himself says so too...'

There is also another reason, among many, why we composers should be frugal and cautious in expressing ourselves, since it isn't sensible to contradict our mistrusted friends, the critics. We should not dismiss their commentaries, since in many cases they reveal his own intentions with greater certainty and wisdom than the composer himself, and are able to isolate with greater clarity and concision the essential inspiration which brought his work into being. And even if this were not so, let us accept them as well, in any case, because then they become the weavers of legend, often more beautiful and more poetic than the truth itself.

Therefore, dear friends, heaven forbid that I should tell you which movement of my *Concierto de Aranjuez* I like the best, or which is the most or the least attractive. I do, of course, know myself – don't be in any doubt! – but prudently and discreetly I prefer to remain silent on the matter. I am going to limit myself, therefore, to telling you about what brought the work into being, and when and how I wrote it.

In September 1938 I was passing through San Sebastián on my way back to France. Someone chosen by God to be a patron of musicians, but who still had to decide to become one, brought Regino Sainz de la Maza and myself together for lunch. We ate well, the wine was not bad either, and the moment was ideal for fantasies and daring ideas. This was also a time full of illusions, in which we Spaniards believed that anything was feasible. Suddenly Regino, in that voluble and determined way of his, said: 'My friend, you must come back with a concerto for guitar and orchestra'; and to soften me up, he added in pathetic tones: 'it's been my lifelong dream!' To ingratiate himself further with me, he went on: 'you are the one destined to do this, like a "chosen one"'! I immediately drank down two glasses of the best Rioja, and exclaimed with the greatest conviction in the world: 'My friend, it's done!' I remember the scene very well, because that evening has remained a happy memory throughout my life, and a moment of calm in those times, which were so turbulent for Spain and so threatening for Europe.

I remember too – I don't know why – (everything to do with the *Concierto de Aranjuez* has remained in my memory) – that one morning, two months later, standing in my little studio in the Rue Saint Jacques in Paris, in the heart of the Latin Quarter, thinking vaguely about the Concerto, since I had become attached to the idea in spite of considering it difficult, I heard within me the entire theme of the 'Adagio', suddenly, without hesitation, and almost as you are about to hear it. And then immediately, with hardly a pause, the theme of the third movement, exactly as it appears in the work.

I quickly realised that the work was done. Our intuition does not deceive us in this. I sketched the outline suggested by the respective themes and wrote the guitar part, together with a first, very rudimentary and uncertain sketch of the orchestral part. Today, when I hear the orchestration of this work, I cannot understand why I had so many doubts and was so dilatory in writing out the different levels of the accompaniment. This contrasted even more with the ease with which I composed the work, and above all with the speed of its conception. If something akin to inspiration, that irresistible and supernatural force, brought me to the 'Adagio' and the final 'Allegro', I came to the first movement through reflection, calculation and will-power. It was the last movement of the three to be composed; and so I finished the work where I should have begun it. For this reason I did not have a clear picture of the whole, except when I had written this first movement. The work was finished in a few months. And the orchestration – a tapestry which, woven around the most elusive of instruments, had itself to form part of it, enclose it, and be within it – was to all intents and purposes complete. It was the spring of 1939. A joyous spring!

The *Concierto de Aranjuez*, written in the spring near the Luxembourg gardens in flower, with the students happily singing, found its final form in Madrid, months later. Only one thing remained to be known, which often kept me awake at night. Could it be played? And would the guitar be heard? The conclusive answer would be given by the hands of Regino. They created the miracle. I, and many others, are very grateful to him.

V

Almost everything that can be written about this Concerto has been said. But the one thing that has not been written, or said, is precisely the thing that the public hopes for, which is for its composer to explain what the music represents, what it means, or what he was thinking of when he created it. But I find myself obliged to say, unfortunately, that the only thing I was thinking was that the said Concerto should turn out as well as possible, that it should give pleasure, and that it should be played a great deal.

What does it represent, or rather, mean? It means whatever any one of us imagines, within the limits suggested by the composer, and which he has tried to convey to his audience – that is to say, a suggestion of times past, of the beautiful gardens of Aranjuez, its fountains, its trees, its birds…

What does this work have, that makes the most diverse audiences, differing in type and size, differing also in their preferences, customs and even nationality, enjoy it with the same delight, the same emotions, the same enthusiasm? Sincerely, I do not know. If I did know, I would have found the ultimate, the panacea – in a word, the philosopher's stone – for my music, and for my success.

The *Concierto de Aranjuez* evokes a vast array of colourful imagery and feelings. Being a history lover, especially of Spanish history, when I created this Concerto I had in mind the courts of Charles IV, a

Bourbon king of 18th-century Spain, whose summer holiday residence was the Palace of Aranjuez. Everything about it is awe-inspiring: its lordly palace; its gardens and fountains; its majestic views. Bearing this in mind while listening to the *Concierto de Aranjuez*, one can clearly visualise the fair ladies, noblemen, toreadors and commoners of the kingdom. Each listener is free to seek his or her own interpretation. Often we are told how the power of this work eases one's soul into profound introspection, releasing so many different feelings and images. It is probably this mysterious power that carries everyone who listens to it in every direction imaginable. If one really stops to think, this Concerto awakens every known feeling and mood – love, joy, war, distress, sadness, poverty, richness, nobility – everything one can think of. If nostalgia could take form, the second movement would be its perfect mold.

Deux berceuses

The most well-known Spanish music has accustomed European audiences to something that is as Spanish as one could wish for, but which is rather singular, in the sense that its inspiration derives, almost without exception, from Andalusia, that extensive region which makes up the south of the Iberian peninsula. The exotic nature of Andalusian songs and dances attracted Spanish composers in the same way that Russian composers were drawn to oriental melodies. But just as one can detect a constant moving away by the Russians from more or less direct folkloric influences, the same thing is happening among young Spanish composers, who are trying to discover new musical styles, new forms of expression which are not bound by popular traditions, however broad these may be, as a result of the great nationalist movements of recent years.

Joaquín Rodrigo's *Deux berceuses* are a result of this change. The first is a suggestive evocation of solitude, in which the nostalgic voice of the cor anglais is heard above a constant background of strings, evoking an endless autumn night.

A harp *glissando* then transports us to the naïve happiness of a childlike spring, expressed in a single theme of markedly Mediterranean character – let us not forget that the composer is from Valencia! – but which is not based on any popular melody. The whole *berceuse* develops as a form of round, led by a lightly-scored and transparent orchestra, a lightness which is emphasised at the end of the *berceuse*, where an ascending scale on the flute above a celesta transforms the theme into a dreamlike Mediterranean springtime.

Zarabanda lejana y villancico

These two compositions, although written some time apart, are nevertheless in the same style and were conceived as though they were a single work. They are evocations of the music of the Spain of the 16th and 17th centuries. The *Zarabanda lejana* was first composed for guitar in 1926, and was dedicated 'To the vihuela of Luis de Milán'. Soon afterwards it was orchestrated by the composer in the form of a dialogue between soloists and orchestra… 'the old sarabande is heard, hidden behind the dense lattice-work of strings, swathed in a haze of mutes…'

The *Villancico*, in contrast to the reserve and refinement of the *Zarabanda*, is written in a simpler, more rustic style. One could say that here the string orchestra reaches the limits of its possibilities in terms of sound. The form is that of a simple sonata rondo, but the writing for strings is extremely difficult. The work was first heard at a private concert in the palace of the Princesse de Polignac; immediately thereafter, in March 1931, at the École Normale; and finally in one of the concerts given by the Orchestre Féminin de Paris.

Per la flor del lliri blau

'Traveller, pause and listen to the song of the blue lily... Can you hear the trumpets of the King? They are summoning the princes to the royal chamber... The King is dying of a strange grief, but before he does, he wants to look for one last time on the blue lily flower. The sound of the martial trumpets awakens echoes in the sleepy mountains, and the three brother princes set out swiftly... They go in search of the longed-for flower. The one who returns with it will gain the whole kingdom as a reward. The youngest of the three rides valiantly and joyfully. He passes through valleys and mountains, rivers and ravines. He rides and rides... ever upwards. The flower is now his. He holds it in his hands, looking at it in ecstasy. He returns joyfully. He again passes through valleys and over mountains.... And arrives. All that remains is to cross the river Arenes.

'Young nobleman. You will not be able to cross, since the daggers of your brothers are awaiting you in the bushes...'

And the prince is dead... The rushes, the reeds, the oleanders weep; the laurel, the agave and the ancient poplar weep; the stones of the ravine, the evening star, the wind in the mountains... Their cries and griefs are raised again and again, day and night...'

Passa, passa, bon germá;	Go on your way, good brother;
passa, passa i no em nomenes,	go on your way and do not heed me,
que m'han mort en riu d'Arenes,	for they have taken my life at the river Arenes,
per la flor del lliri blau...	for the flower of the blue lily...

This work was composed for a competition organised by the Círculo de Bellas Artes in Valencia in July 1934 and was unanimously awarded the first prize.

It is inspired by an old Catalan/Valencian song, the words of which, written in the Valencian dialect, are by the composer himself. They tell, somewhat freely, a traditional legend. The folksong does not appear until the end of the work, where it appears successively in fifths throughout all the instruments of the orchestra: double bassoon, bass clarinet, cor anglais, bassoon, flutes, oboes and clarinets, horns, violins and finally, brass.

With echoes of another popular song, the three side-drums are included to form the second theme of the work. The main inspirational element of the composition is the original theme, which is played by the viola in a rhapsodic style.

The whole work has the character of a mediaeval legend, not without a certain romanticism. The work was extremely successful at its first performance, to the extent of being repeated in the following concert. It is in the repertoire of a number of orchestras.

Homenaje a 'La tempranica'

I think of this short composition as something closely related to the *Concierto de Aranjuez*. In fact, this work was composed like the latter in Paris in the spring of 1939, and sometimes there occur in this world of music – as in the distant world of stars – scraps detached from larger compositions which circle within the same orbit. They are like a parenthesis of another work, unable to escape from the composer's primary and overriding preoccupation.

Nevertheless there is a tendency here which, although begun in a previous work – the 'Homenaje a Chueca' for piano (*Caleseras*) – would continue to have great importance in later compositions such as the *Concierto galante* for 'cello, or the *Sonatas de Castilla*. I am referring to my intention of inserting turns of phrase or rhythmic patterns from our *zarzuela* traditions into symphonic music. A small but characteristic melodic phrase from Giménez's masterpiece is the origin of this brief homage, which comprises a 'lento' (a prelude) and an 'allegro' (a dance), forming in this way a kind of small overture to our most representative *zarzuela*.

Concierto heroico

Rodrigo's review of the première of the Concierto heroico, *given on the 7th May 1942 by Leopoldo Querol and the Orquesta Nacional, conducted by Bartolomé Pérez Casas.*

Your correspondent has to be brief in his commentary on what was for him the memorable concert given yesterday in the Teatro Español. He feels himself too involved in the occasion to write at his ease, or to praise sufficiently those responsible for the success.

But I do wish to repeat the words which, at the request of my friend Carlos del Pozo, I uttered yesterday to the microphone, a few moments after the performance of my Concerto, adding some more general comments about the genesis of this most recent work of mine.

Above all I must pay a warm tribute to Maestro Pérez Casas, in the following very simple but utterly justified words: 'Entrusting to the Maestro the first performance of a work is to receive in return an absolute guarantee of success, and, what is even more important, to feel oneself interpreted in the most subtly inspired of ways, including in those intentions – often just allusions – which the artist wishes unconsciously to express, and of which even he himself is unaware.' Maestro Pérez Casas is able to allow himself what foolish people might call the 'sacrifice of his own success'; as though triumphs could be distinguished, when it is a question of collaboration in a concerto! Pérez Casas is above all that; but even so, one should not draw less attention to it, or be less grateful to him. He has dedicated the greater part of his time to working out a score which is not at all easy, full of hidden references, and has done so with an understanding and – what is even more important – an affection in which the exemplary modesty of this extraordinary musician has been made clear.

As far as Leopoldo Querol is concerned, a brotherly friendship which has lasted over twenty-five years has made this shared success all the more happy and joyous for me. In my work he has found ample scope to demonstrate his formidable technique, rhythmic drive, and that remarkable musical judgement on which he draws to make possible the association of his name with so many first performances of the most diverse and unusual works.

In addition, he played the work with the enthusiasm which comes from long and impatient anticipation. In fact, after the success of this same artist with Ravel's Concerto, some ten or twelve years ago, and which confirmed his outstanding qualities, it became very common both here and elsewhere to write concertos for the piano. There was no composer who, after that triumph, did not think of 'taking on' Querol. I myself as well, of course, and the first of all.

The promise of a 'concerto' dates exactly from 1933, the year of my first jottings for such a work. In the winter of 1935 I wrote a first movement, completely orchestrated, and in the summer of the same year, in Salzburg, I composed and orchestrated the second movement. The years passed, and our Civil War broke out. Many things changed, and times also change artists, a fair recompense for when it is the latter who change the times. Having written the *Concierto de Aranjuez* for Sainz de la Maza, I decided to fulfil my promise to Querol, but what I had composed by then, more than half the work, I didn't like, and even more than not liking it, it didn't satisfy me. I wanted to write a different work, and in the spring of 1940, I began to make notes for nothing less than a 'heroic concerto'.

It was easy for me to see that the terms 'concerto' and 'heroic' were completely opposed and antithetical; but for that very reason I undertook the composition of the work with greater enthusiasm, since at times giving oneself problems to solve is enjoyable and even useful. What has cost me the most in this work has been finding the character and trying to give a particular context to each movement, and, above all, within the unity imposed by the title, trying to resolve those opposing terms, 'concerto' and 'heroic'. I have tried to write a 'concerto', and music, with heroic ambitions, wishing to awake in the listener a series of poetic images, with the titles of the different movements not even hinting at any allusions, since that would have been a flagrant betrayal of the 'concerto', one of the purest, most abstract and decorative musical forms. I also wanted the piano to be the 'hero' and the orchestra not to serve it as an accompaniment, nor background, but rather as a stimulus, a spur, to make possible its pianistic endeavours – something like the reason for and justification of the undertaking. I do not know if I have succeeded. I do know that this is the work I have written with the greatest speed, within the summer of 1942. But with greater anxiety than any other work of mine.

All I can say is that I have enjoyed myself hugely, and in saying this I am remembering the admirable words of Manuel de Falla, when in the Prologue to Joaquín Turina's *Enciclopedia abreviada de la música* he writes: 'One should compose with happiness, with joy, because he who takes pleasure in his profession is likely to give pleasure to others.'

To judge from the applause and reception of my work yesterday, which I shall never forget, I do believe that the audience did enjoy itself, and it is unnecessary to say that, when Falla alluded to enjoyment, he was speaking of the pleasure, the emotion an artist feels, when he sees his work before him, being able to contemplate it and touch it at his leisure, feeling the pure and intimate sense of seeing, or believing to see in it, some realised and longed-for desire.

There only remains for me – with the greatest pleasure – to thank the Orquesta Nacional. It is not because of my personal involvement that I say that it is the best orchestra in Spain; the players know that very well. But it is important that a national orchestra should achieve the real independence it must have, and our best means of assuring musical excellence is to provide the financial support needed, which other countries have given their orchestras for a long time. Every player excelled himself in the performance of my work, as they did in the remainder of the programme, made up of works by three musical giants: *Fingal's Cave*, by Mendelssohn, excerpts from *Die Meistersinger* by Wagner, and the 'Pathétique' Symphony by Tchaikovsky. These works were a personal triumph for Maestro Pérez Casas; and a quiet satisfaction was experienced by everyone, hearing the orchestra directed by the finest conductor in Spain.

Concierto de estío

We should not seek or hope to find in the *Concierto de estío*, in spite of its title, preconceived intentions or direct allusions, as could be done with the *Concierto heroico*, which was inspired by a poetic concept. However, the conscious or implicit suggestiveness which is inevitably indicated by the adoption of a general title of this kind, and the fact of having had recourse to the titles 'Preludio', 'Siciliana' and 'Rondino' for the three movements – terms unequivocally typical of a style, a form and even a period – reveal the composer's intention, and the aesthetic stance, of a work linked with emblems beloved of Vivaldi, and familiar from his work.

In the *Concierto de estío*, composed in the fields and beneath the sun of my country, there are, however, no elements of popular music, except in the 'Rondino', where, even though well disguised, it is not difficult to discover a Catalan influence. In the 'Preludio', too, in its second theme, played by the woodwind, there are traces of the influence of popular dance-forms. In spite of these light touches of popular music, which are to be found in every Spanish musical composition, intentionally or not, the themes of the *Concierto de estío* are taken from elements purified and accredited through long use in the most aristocratic forms of music.

The first movement of the Concerto follows the traditional form, leaving out, as in earlier concertos, the double exposition. The 'Siciliana' is based on a single theme, and here one can detect a feature latent in my work, and clearly present in the *Concierto heroico*, the variation form. In this movement, as Sainz de la Maza has observed, an intense game is played between the 'Siciliana' theme and the opening theme of the work, a relationship which is resolved in the cadenza. The 'Rondino', at least in its elaboration and creation, is the most consciously composed part of the work. I wanted to trace with its theme a kind of formal harmonic circle, so that the 'refrain' should revolve around a pre-established plan – ten successive appearances of the theme, without an obvious ending, and without any other episode being inserted amongst these ten repetitions. These appear more as 'variants' than 'variations', since the word 'variation' could seem rather pretentious here. The violin pirouettes upon harmonic bases made up of the tonic, subdominant and dominant, and around it the other instruments travel in sudden flights to sometimes distant tonalities, but always subject to the prevailing tonal scheme, drawing a magic circle which is repeated three times.

As far as the spirit of the work is concerned, I have tried to give new life to the concerto form prior to Mozart and Haydn. The intention, I am aware, is very ambitious; and, therefore, I do not know if I have been successful.

Capriccio
Ofrenda a Pablo Sarasate

The *Capriccio* for violin is my most ambitious work for a solo instrument since the *Preludio al gallo mañanero*, for piano. It was conceived in Santander in the summer of 1944 and finished in Madrid, exactly a year ago. The piece arose from a conversation I had with Antonio de las Heras in which we planned the idea of weaving a garland for Sarasate on the microphones of Radio Madrid, with the intention of celebrating the first centenary of the birth of our great violinist.

This 'Offering to Sarasate' comes immediately after the *Concierto de estío*. These two violin works, with the *Dos esbozos* for violin and piano, form the bridge beneath which all my music still lightly flows.

Whenever a composer insists on his preference for a particular musical form, or better still, as in this case, a particular instrument, (especially if this insistence is followed through), we must look for the reason for the preference, which the chance of the inspiration of the moment brings about. And then, perhaps we would be able to find a particular intention, or perhaps some lack of satisfaction. There is something of all that in this *Capriccio* of mine.

When I finished the *Concierto de estío* I realised I had only reached the half-way point of the road I was following. To have continued with another 'concerto' in those circumstances would have been tiresome, as it is very easy to fall into inevitable pedantry. And also, it is very pleasant to be called the 'composer of the three Concertos'! However, it was necessary to repeat certain formulas and intentions which were not very well demonstrated in the *Concierto de estío*. But is it possible to write an attractive violin piece, whose unadorned elegance brings together the magic of the solo instrument and the attraction of musical ensemble, without the tedious halter of its tutor, the piano, getting in the way? On the other hand, the piano of Andalusia, virtually exhausted by guitaristic effects, presents to a young composer the great mountain range of Albéniz's *Iberia*, an almost impenetrable barrier, which, emerging from the towering musical heritage of Spain, threatens to close off all pianistic horizons. But it is worth transplanting that famous musical style, which is so Spanish, to infuse or inject that essence into other mediums, atmospheres, or agents of sound. And there is nothing more appropriate to rejuvenating the old, worn-out piano than by transforming it into a violin, an instrument which has been able to keep its youthfulness without renouncing the modest attire of its four strings, singing 'serenades' to the moon, and hiding itself for more than a hundred years beneath the disguise of the most adorable triviality.

So let us open the book of the old magical charms of the guitar, with its eternally mysterious formulas of Spanish music, and make them gallop on this 'fleet-footed instrument', the violin, a charger with neither bridle nor harness, all purity of line and purity of speed, now that it is no longer encumbered by that heavy rider, the cold and noble piano.

A l'ombre de Torre Bermeja

A l'ombre de Torre Bermeja was written as a posthumous homage to someone who was both a great pianist and a great pioneer of contemporary Spanish and European music, the Catalan pianist Ricardo Viñes, who died some years ago, in Barcelona. A number of us composed a series of works in his memory, in gratitude for what he had done for us, and I wrote a kind of commentary, a paraphrase of a work by Albéniz from his early period, called *Torre Bermeja*.[1] In particular because Ricardo Viñes liked the piece very much and played it in a quite wonderful way. So, I wrote a form of commentary on the work. I did not use any themes from it, but I was inspired to some extent by its atmosphere, in so far as its essence was concerned. And I also called it '*A l'ombre de Torre Bermeja*', that is, in the 'shadow' of Torre Bermeja, partly in French, partly in Spanish, recalling in this way that Albéniz once did the same in his early period, giving his works bilingual titles. Ricardo Viñes had also been, in fact, a Spanish and in some ways a French pianist too.

This idea, something of an intellectual exercise, has given me quite a few surprises. For example, when the work was published and already on sale, the editor telephoned me in an agitated state to say: 'Maestro, forgive me, but you write "hombre" with an "h"'! The man was of course rather perplexed.[2] And the title was always translated badly, for some reason. The other day I received a programme of a concert in Germany, where it was played with the title: 'In the shade of the reddish bull'. [3] Very strange! And there are many similar examples which I could relate. The Torre Bermeja, as you know, served as a prison for many years, and some critics have imagined that I was inspired by the sufferings of the prisoners in the jails there. No, no, not at all. It is in fact a literary reference, and I am sure that Ricardo Viñes himself would have enjoyed sleeping in the shade of this Torre Bermeja, in Granada. You will hear at the end of the piece that there are some bells tolling in his memory, and the themes, without having a note of Albéniz in them, do bring to mind somewhat the first period of that composer's music.

[1] The 'Torre Bemeja' is a fortress situated on a hill overlooking the Alhambra in Granada.

[2] The editor had mistaken the French word 'ombre' (shade) for the Spanish 'hombre' (man).

[3] The writer of the programme notes had confused 'torre' (tower) with 'toro' (bull).

Ausencias de Dulcinea

This symphonic poem is based on the poetic composition of Cervantes entitled 'Árboles, hierbas y plantas'. Three styles, one could even say three moods, are present in this work, following one another almost without interruption: the opening fanfares, the five notes of the oboes and 'cellos taken from a ballad; the orchestra's mockery of some of Don Quixote's utterances; and finally the lyrical passage which is heard at the end of each verse.

The composer has eliminated from this composition any allusion to or picturesque description of place and atmosphere: no streams or waving branches, no mountains of the Sierra Morena; just Don Quixote, raising his voice to declaim his sorrows to the surrounding solitude, taking as his witnesses 'trees, herbs and plants'. The orchestra underlines his singing, just as it also expresses laughter or mockery on hearing the verses of the poem, representing in this way an invisible chorus of disrespectful yokels. Finally, there is the constant obsession of Don Quixote: Dulcinea, whose voice reaches him from the four points of the compass – thus explaining the composer's need for four soprano voices.

Apart from the themes outlined here, it is useful to point out occasional allusions to the popular ballad 'Mambrú se va a la guerra', an ironic evocation of those knights-errant represented by Don Quixote himself.

The poem by Cervantes which is glossed in this work by the composer is as follows:

Árboles, yerbas y plantas	Trees, herbs and plants
que en este sitio estáis,	which are present in this place,
tan altos, verdes y tantas,	so tall and green, so numerous,
si de mi mal no os holgáis,	if you do not rejoice at my wretchedness,
escuchad mis quejas santas.	then listen to my noble complaint.
Mi dolor no os alborote,	May my grief not shock you,
aunque más terrible sea;	no matter how terrible it seems;
pues, por pagaros escote,	since, to share it with you,
aquí lloró don Quijote	it was here that Don Quixote wept

ausencias de Dulcinea	for the absence of Dulcinea
del Toboso.	del Toboso.
Buscando las aventuras	Seeking adventures
por entre las duras peñas,	amongst the harsh rocks,
maldiciendo entrañas duras,	cursing that hard heart,
que entre riscos y entre breñas	amidst crags and brambles
halla el triste desventuras,	the wretched one finds misfortune.
hirióle amor con un azote,	Love wounded him with its whip,
no con su blanda correa;	not with soft ribbons,
y en tocándole el cogote,	and, cut to the quick,
aquí lloró don Quijote	it was here that Don Quixote wept
ausencias de Dulcinea	for the absence of Dulcinea
del Toboso.	del Toboso.

II

It is certainly true that some eighty per cent of Spanish music of the last seventy-five years is inspired by dance and popular song, with a certain oriental colouring. All this music is, therefore, either 'dance', or a means by which one can express oneself without that 'picturesqueness' which can seem facile. Our music is almost always rather poematic, but rather than literary virtues we can find in this poetry choreographic qualities of great evocative power. From all this one can understand the very insignificant place that sonatas and symphonies have in our music, forms which have always been avoided by our composers.

I belong to a generation of musicians who felt the need to react strongly against the excesses of 'costumbrismo', and while not distancing myself from the general currents in this renaissance of our music, I have modestly tried to link it with matters of more universal form.

Ausencias de Dulcinea is a work belonging to the music inspired by *Don Quijote de la Mancha*. There have been many works written on this theme. I will just mention the one which opened a new way forward for Spanish music, Manuel de Falla's *El retablo de Maese Pedro*. From this work onwards, we Spanish composers began to search for older traditions, based on Castilian music of the 16th century. My work is a form of 'poem' for bass solo, four sopranos and orchestra. It is inspired by the verses written by Don Quixote in the Sierra Morena, sometimes exalted and grandiloquent, at others comic, even grotesque. Each of the stanzas into which the poem is divided ends with an invocation to Dulcinea del Toboso. It is then that the voice of Dulcinea is heard, like an obsession, sounding from all four points of the compass, always repeating the word 'Dulcinea'. The music follows the strangeness of the poem, and is full of chivalresque themes, based clearly on madrigal origins.

III

By the year 1925 I had already set ancient texts by some of our poets, such as the Marqués de Santillana, and later, Gil Vicente. I would never have set Cervantes to music, since literary critics thought him a poor poet. But it came about that a national competition was organised to mark the fourth centenary of Cervantes's birth, with a substantial prize. I immediately forgot my fear of Cervantes's poetry! The organisers of the competition published two poems which might be chosen. One, which was very well known, and another one, which I chose because I had already read it (I assure you that I really have read *Don Quijote!*). Although very difficult, it was more interesting for me, given my intuitions as a composer.

But nothing came to me, and in something of a state just three weeks before the closing date of the competition, I suddenly began to conceive ideas for a symphonic poem, which I then wrote very quickly. Once the ideal internal structure emerges, composing is very easy for me. And I won the prize!

The work is a development along lines first established in my songs, *Muy graciosa es la doncella*, *Serranilla* and *Romance anónimo*. These make clear a path which led to *Cántico de la esposa*, continuing to some extent with *El lirio azul*, and with the *Concierto heroico* in 1942, finally reaching this work in 1948, which, according to the critics, marks a definitive moment in my music.

Every country's composer writes what he feels, or what he is able to write, depending on the external possibilities which are available to him. (There are amazing possibilities abroad, where they have access to things we Spaniards are not able to deploy). He uses every orchestral instrument available at the time, together with those things which the work inspires in him. The character of Don Quixote suggests a bass voice, or, instrumentally, a 'cello, going down to bottom F – though it is not a good idea to write many such notes to be sung. I made the simple mistake of doing so, and some basses refuse to sing them!

The reason why *Ausencias de Dulcinea* has four female voices is because of the symbolism of the work. Don Quixote goes to the Sierra Morena to do penance, following the knightly example of Amadís. In fact he does many silly things. The worst of his madness is to write poems and carve them on those cork trees which are as hard as the head of Don Quixote himself. And this is one of those poems.

The poem has three verses, each of them divided into two five-line stanzas – the first chivalric in nature and the second developing without a break into celebratory, ironic or ridiculous style, like Don Quixote himself. I do not think it is true that this is bad poetry. In the music the extra lines are sung by the four female voices, going from a mezzo up to a high D, enveloping the knight. The poetry is by turns heroic and burlesque, sung by both the knight and the voices around him. The madrigal-like part of the work is sung by the four female voices, generally in counterpoint. Don Quixote always sings seriously, in a knightly manner, while the voices of Dulcinea sound almost like a madrigal. The orchestra's music is at times like the latter, at others it is in a burlesque style.

There is an introduction, then a short verse, followed by the female voices. The second verse is shared between Don Quixote, the other voices and the orchestra. To finish, there is a third verse and coda, and the composer's decision to repeat the first verse, with the knight's self-glorification, followed by a *forte* chord. At this point everything disappears, leaving only the sound of the invocatory voices of Dulcinea.

The work ends pianissimo in C major, on an interrupted cadence.

Cuatro madrigales amatorios

Manuel de Falla's *El retablo de Maese Pedro* brought the love for and the inspiration of the Renaissance music of the Spanish *Cancioneros* to the composers who followed him. No one has studied and felt that music more than Joaquín Rodrigo, who has always searched within popular traditions for the essential 'perfume' rather than the historical 'fact'. If in the *Romance de la Infantina de Francia* he reveals to us his personal vision of a mood free from the influence of the past, in the *Cuatro madrigales amatorios* the compositions have been created upon four particular melodies. Once again the composer completely avoids all folkloric erudition in order to elaborate the themes freely, to deal with them as though they are his own. In this he does not follow the example of Falla in his *Siete canciones populares españolas*. Falla recreates popular music from essentially folkloric material, with the greatest respect for the melodies. This is not the case with Rodrigo in 'De los álamos vengo, madre' or '¿De dónde venís, amore', the two happy songs. The other two, 'Vos me matasteis' and '¿Con qué la lavaré?' have a quite different colouring, filled with intense melancholy and the deepest sadness.

Concierto en modo galante

This Concerto was commissioned by the Spanish 'cellist, Gaspar Cassadó, and following its première in Madrid in 1949 it was played throughout Europe with great success.

The work is divided into three movements: 'Allegretto grazioso', 'Adagietto' and 'Rondo giocoso'. All its themes, though totally the invention of the composer, make constant allusion to *boleros*, *panaderos* and *zapateados*, Spanish dances which were very much in vogue in the second half of the 19th century. This explains the title 'galante', even though the work is absolutely of our own time in its harmonic language, its contemporary writing for the 'cello, and its sparkling orchestration.

From its very first notes this Concerto takes us to Spain, but without recourse to superficial impressions of more or less Andalusian music, a region which until very recently monopolised the whole of Spanish music, and against whose overly familiar procedures contemporary Spanish composers have reacted strongly.

In the first movement there is a brief introduction in which, over a 'cello ostinato, all the instruments appear which make up the orchestra: two flutes, two oboes, two clarinets, two bassoons, two horns, two trumpets, and strings. The solo instrument then introduces the first theme in F major, the key of the work, accompanied by pizzicato strings. After a secondary, though characteristic, motif, the second theme is introduced, in A major, in the style of a courtly minuet, in which the 'cello alternates with a stately fanfare of piccolos and muted trumpets. These themes introduce elements of the second part of the movement, in a *panadero* style. And after a very dynamic section in which the themes are presented in various superimposed keys, there comes the cadenza, after which all the themes are recapitulated in classical style, the movement ending with a clear reminder of the introduction.

The second movement, in F minor, presents a single-themed 'arietta', whose basis is the same as that which formed the first theme of the first movement. This 'arietta' is interrupted by a trio, or central section, in which pastoral sounds suggest a landscape of northern Spain. This is resolved in the swirls of an Asturian *fandango*, ending the movement with the recapitulation of the short 'arietta' and the pastoral theme, bringing the second movement to an end pianissimo.

The third movement, totally *zapateado* in style, is written in the form of a rondo. The refrain is presented by the 'cello and is then repeated by the 'tutti', alternating, as in the rondo form, with a certain number of 'couplets' in which the 'cello elegantly leaps and skips, followed in its continuous pirouettes by the orchestra, which brings the *Concierto en modo galante* to an end on a series of short, sharp chords.

Dos canciones sefardíes del siglo XV

The journal *Sefarad* has offered me the chance to publish the stylised harmonisation, as we might say, of *Dos canciones sefardíes*, which I have composed for four- or six-part chorus.

Sephardic Jews have created for us a popular form of song which, having a less evolved character than our own, offers us a field of comparison which allows for a very good, or at least an historical, understanding of our own popular music. I do not know to what point and with what focus one is able to undertake this study, but thanks to the published collections we now have, it can be made with the appropriate guarantees.

One of these collections was made directly by Manrique de Lara and given to me by Don Ramón Menéndez Pidal, and from it I have selected two, among many such songs, in order to subject them to the elaboration of choral arrangement. In spite of what is often assumed, the harmonisation of a popular song is not easy. One is faced immediately with the grave problem involved in reconciling a 'light' musical form with a more 'serious' one. Popular song, especially popular for us in our own time, comes free of formal prejudices, since it flourished in countries in which art was hardly cultivated or even possible, and in centuries in which the serious artistic forms of Western music were still fighting to impose themselves. A narrative, or an expression of feeling, did not need to be, or was not accompanied by, anything other than the lightest support, the most limited accompaniment, if it was a ballad, or even less if it was just a lyric, since in both cases its own direct significance was sufficient.

Later, the Western world was overtaken by the marvellous invention of polyphony, which first awakened and then demanded a way of listening to music (not just hearing it, which would be less interesting), a requirement and a custom which totally separates us from the East. The two worlds and the two conceptions of music clash with each other, especially when attempts are made to harmonise the popular song. And this is the problem – how to yoke the charger of the popular song to the carriage of polyphony. The answer, if it exists, would seem to be to prefer 'atmosphere' to something academic. That is, to try to situate the song in what seems to be its milieu, to place it there by recreating its world, aims which are more feasible when we accompany the song with one or more instruments than when we try to adapt it for a choir of singers, in spite of what we might at first think.

This was my wish on tackling the problem, knowing that there would always be an inherent difficulty here. Therefore, and following my intention to enclose the folkloric element in a suitable atmosphere, I have deployed the sopranos in four voice parts to tell the story of the king's son's illness ('Malato estaba el hijo del rey') ('The son of the king is gravely ill'), with the simple expressiveness of a children's round or game. There is then a more emotional quality to the music, as the song becomes more individual, accompanied by an almost funerary pedal note in the men's voices, beneath the insistently repeated 'que non salva, non salvaba' ('he cannot be saved') of the contraltos.

The second piece is a hunting song: 'El rey que mucho madruga, donde la caza se iba', ('The king rises early to go hunting'). The melody breaks out in the vibrant voices of the tenors, and following them, as though in pursuit, come the various components of the choir: basses, contraltos and sopranos, who eventually form themselves into two groups singing in different and opposing keys, with the brightness of hunting horns.

We must not forget, therefore, that we are attempting to evoke a world, the world of the song, when we try to put harmonies to it. Only in this way and with this desire can we solve the great antithesis, even the grave sin, of imprisoning ancient song-forms, for our own pleasure, within the cage of our profession as Western composers.

II

Within the rich and varied folklore of Spain, the collection of songs which the Hebrews of this country have kept with the utmost care, down to our own times, enclose a particular delight. In spite of the passage of years – many centuries, in fact – they reveal deeply Spanish traits, mixed with a clear orientalism, which is also a large part, it must be said, of Spanish music itself.

The first of these two songs, 'Malato está el hijo del rey', alludes, without doubt, to the illness and death of Prince Don Juan, the only child of the Catholic Monarchs, Ferdinand and Isabella.

Malato está el hijo del rey	The son of the king is gravely ill.
Malato que no salvaba.	So ill he will not survive.
Siete doctores lo miran,	Seven doctors attend to him,
Los mejores de Granada.	The finest in Granada.
Siete doctores lo miran,	Seven doctors attend to him,
Los mejores de Granada.	The finest in Granada.
Cien ya suben, cien ya baxan,	A hundred have come, a hundred have gone,
Ninguno le hace nada.	Not one has helped him.

The first and second lines are sung, first, by the women's voices, divided into three parts for the first line and four for the second. This second line is repeated by the sopranos against a gloomy background of strange harmonies, given to the men's voices, while the contraltos sing 'que non salva, non salvaba' in a sinister way.

The second song, 'El rey que mucho madruga', is composed like a hunting call. The very brief text is as follows:

El rey que mucho madruga	The king rises early
Donde la caza se iba.	To go hunting.

Bitonal combinations, very effective in choral writing, crackle along happily, while the voices follow one another in canon, imitating a hunt.

Concierto serenata

The happy, bell-like sounds of the harp, and its suitability for diatonic music – that is, clear and simple – suggested to me a concerto which would be like a message to young people, awakening echoes of customs and celebrations from times past – hence the title, *Concierto serenata*. This is why the work is based in that Spanish 19th century which we invented musically, and are still busy reconstructing through the works of Padre Soler and Barbieri.

The first movement of the *Concierto serenata*, 'Estudiantina' ('Allegro') is faithful to the form of the first movement of the classical concerto, although unlike what occurs in the great period of the concerto, the second theme, played by the orchestra, is hardly significant; rather than a theme, it is a brief refrain. The whole movement develops in the form of a march, and no-one should be surprised that in its development, as should occur in any 'estudiantina', one will hear the occasional scrap of well-known music.

The second movement, 'Intermezzo con aria', is an 'arietta' in canonic form, sung by the harp, which is interrupted by a fugal 'allegretto', which nevertheless allows the theme of the 'aria' to end pianissimo, after the whole orchestra has given full expression to its emotion.

The third movement, 'Sarao' ('Allegro vivace') is composed in the form of a rondo, that is, a principal theme which alternates with other secondary themes, although these themes become significant in their own right.

I have tried to achieve something very difficult – that everything should be light, clear and joyous, like the child soul of the harp itself, and like a 'Concert Serenade'.

Música para un códice salmantino
or
The Composer and his Work

Amongst the many new and extraordinary experiences for the human being of our time I should like to emphasise the one which consists in nothing less than the fact that man has heard and listened to himself. A remarkable invention has been able to capture for ever in inexplicable grooves and magnetic strips the voice, the words and the song of man. And man has been able to hear himself, and have before him a hitherto impossible image of himself.

I do not know what Eve thought when for the first time she was able to look at herself, and contemplate herself, on the day when the waters, themselves absorbed, reflected back the first face of a woman. But I imagine the effect was the same; Eve did not recognise herself. She did not recognise herself in the clearest possible mirror of those clearest waters, just as none of us have recognised ourselves after the extraordinary experience of hearing ourselves for the first time. This experience is by its very nature disconcerting, but what is even more so is the immediate consequence which probably repeats the distressing vision. We do not recognise ourselves, and we do not *like* ourselves. We don't like ourselves because we had an innate and perhaps necessary overestimation of ourselves; in other words, our vanity has been wounded. And all this confirms the opinion of psychologists who, playing with the apparent paradox, maintain that it is easier to know others than to know oneself.

The exterior aspect and its internal manifestation, the face and the voice – what is commonly called the 'mirror of the soul' and that other thing which I would call the echo of its very substance, the voice – have been subjected to the same tests. And man does not recognise himself, and when he looks, he feels mortified because he doesn't like himself, because he thought himself much better.

We could multiply or repeat in gradations of a lesser category the vicissitudes of one's self-examination, whenever we distance ourselves from ourselves, or from our own works or even our own actions. The painter standing back from his canvas, the composer listening to his music interpreted by others, feels an inexpressible disappointment

207

that what he has created seems somehow different. If this is so, how can we be our own critics? And yet, the creator's function requires vigilance, the discrimination provided by technical knowledge, his innate acquired taste, and his instinct, which in the arts is replaced by sensibility. It is from this need and that incapacity that I believe the terrible doubt is born which assails the creator's courage concerning the need for, or the significance of, his art.

As for me, whenever I have tried to say something about my modest works, I stand perplexed before the latest composition, with its ink barely dry, which time has not passed over nor conferred any sense of 'otherness' to it.

But these professions of humility are worth nothing, or very little. Our determination, also valid and necessary, will make us affirm, finally, that we do indeed know something about ourselves; and even that we know about our intentions and desires, and that we *can* say something about our works – what we have tried to achieve, how we have tried to do it, and what our music is, formally. Information which, even if not precise enough for the casual academic researcher – if we do not try to deceive him by deceiving ourselves – can save him searches and assumptions which can also be diverted or lost in the labyrinth of the intentions and desires of the artist.

II

In truth, if I had not received from my very good friend Don Antonio Tovar, the Rector of Salamanca University, the suggestion that I should write a form of cantata to mark the end of the activities commemorating the seventh centenary of the foundation of the University, I would never have set my hand to the poetry of Miguel de Unamuno, in spite of considering him to be one of the greatest contemporary poets of Castile.

But was it possible to try and fulfil such a prestigious commission – a double honour now – to join together Salamanca and its university with Unamuno? With the greatest respect and the humblest devotion I decided to approach the verses of Don Miguel – or, as he might have said rather better, to 'people the world of his poetry with ghostly sounds'. Strangely, though, Unamuno did not like any arts which dwell in magic castles, and – can music be found in them? – as far as my powers are able, I have tried to expel them. But I am very much afraid that a few of those spirits which the bard of Salamanca so feared have, in spite of everything, slipped through my fingers.

And so, with that intention, I copied the ode to Salamanca which begins:

Alto soto de torres que al ponerse	Tall grove of towers which, as the sun sets
tras las encinas que el celaje esmalta...	behind the oak trees which embellish the sky...

and from which I selected some verses. Goodness me! I have never applied myself with such attention and such devotion to the syntaxis and the prosody of a text – which I do not normally think about in such a way – as to this one. Don Miguel, this is the best I can do!

The elevated nature of the poetry, its noble tone and personal voice, was ideally expressed in the voice of a bass soloist. But at times the verse gives way to a more lyrical form of expression. Oh, those fantasies, Don Miguel! And here I found a way to introduce a four-voice chorus, to add certain elements to the actual situation – celebrations for the ending of an anniversary marking seven centuries. But how to recall King Alfonso the Wise, the founder of the university? Eleven very disparate instruments – piccolo, flute, cor anglais, horn, trumpet and five-part strings – introduce, play and develop a musical phrase in the form of an introit, a *Deo gratias*, such as God himself might have suggested to the poor minstrel devoted to his arduous tasks.

But one instrument has not been mentioned – the harp, which punctuates and colours the line sung by the bass soloist, sustaining it in a mood of austere nobility. Salamanca, the halls of its university, and the sun which lights up the golden stones of its high towers, are saluted by sonorous choral fanfares, which prolong the echoes of those same lecture halls in which 'the students learnt of love.'

III

This work, dated the 19th September 1953 in Torrelodones, belongs to the broad category of 'cantata', and was written to commemorate the seven-hundredth anniversary of the founding of the University of Salamanca.

As can be seen from the work's title in the score, it is written for a bass soloist, four-voice mixed choir, and eleven instruments: two violins, viola, 'cello, doublebass, piccolo, flute, cor anglais, horn, trumpet and harp. It will escape no-one's attention, therefore, that this limited but colourful assembly of instruments which accompanies the protagonist of the 'cantata', the bass soloist and, in its turn, the choir which is both commentator and opponent – all explain the composer's principal intention or aim – evocation.

The genealogy of this composition (others more qualified than I will confirm this) begins with my *Cantiga* on verses by Gil Vicente from 1925, reaching a climax in the setting I made of part of the *Cántico espiritual* of San Juan de la Cruz, to then finally emerge in *Ausencias de Dulcinea*, to words from *Don Quijote de la Mancha*. But I believe these works are as unlike each other as possible.

The themes of the work consist of what we might call three elements. One particular theme with the atmosphere of a 'cantiga' and of a purely instrumental character begins the 'cantata'. It may also appear later in the voice parts, but always understood as an additional colouring to the instrumental essence of the 'cantata'.

Secondly, an air, or perhaps a chant, entrusted to the singer. Third, a melodic atmosphere shared between Gregorian cadences and Castilian popular song. The musical basis of the harmony is the perfect chord, which rises gently to the major seventh which punctuates the saphic cadences of Unamuno's verse. This whole harmonic atmosphere is held within the same mood until the end, stretched upon the clash of equivocal tonality, whose uncertainty is accentuated by the sonorous elements employed.

The form or structure of the composition, which lasts for about twelve minutes, follows more or less the form of the 'motet', as usually occurs in all vocal compositions. However, an occasional lyrical episode gives the work a few brief reappearances of themes which, alongside the actual theme of the work, achieves, I believe, that unity to which we are accustomed, as a result of the success of those musical forms which we might generously call 'modern'. Nevertheless, the 'cantata' opens with what I have called an 'introit', a very real *Deo*

210

gratias that God has allowed us to be part of this commemoration. It consists of a canon at the octave and in eight parts (although in good contrapuntal theory it should be more). I conceived this Introit as a form of minstrelsy which might have been invented by that master of the organ to whom King Don Sancho entrusted the teaching of music in this university. Purely instrumental music, and of an intended objectivity or abstraction in sound.

The call of the cuckoo (the composer's familiar signature), the sonorous fanfares which salute Salamanca and its halls, or the distant sound of the sopranos, responding to the magic of student love, which the harp accompanies with faint reminiscences of earlier music, are decorative elements which complete the composer's intention: to *evoke*.

Fantasía para un gentilhombre

For the composition of the *Fantasía para un gentilhombre*, I took my inspiration from Gaspar Sanz's *Instrucción de música sobre la guitarra española*, the first published guitar manual, but I used the contents of this work very freely. A proof of this is that from six minutes of Sanz's music I composed an orchestral work which lasts twenty. The titles of the different movements, both ancient and modern, are as follows: 'Villano', 'Ricercar', 'Españoleta y toques de la Caballería de Nápoles', 'Danza de las hachas' and 'Canario'.

I have written as follows about the *Fantasía*. 'One day, when passing through Madrid, Andrés Segovia invited me to write a work for him for the guitar. The form of it or its title were not important; he simply told me that he would prefer it to be with a small orchestra.'

In my music there are influences, not wholly unfortunate, from the golden age of our music, especially that backbone which unites the 16th with the 17th century in our vocal and instrumental music (*Cuatro madrigales amatorios*), together with attempts to capture the spirit of Scarlatti via Padre Soler. The latter intention seemed to me some years ago a way of creating for myself a 'neoclassical' style, so it was similarly important to gather up in this subtle web the loose ends of the 17th century. And for that it was necessary to turn to Gaspar Sanz, a musician in whom we can see the spirit of a moribund century at a crossroads with the spirit of the century to come – sentiment encountering reason.

All of this, although only in a limited way, is undoubtedly to be found in the work of Gaspar Sanz, the first musician to ennoble the guitar, which had previously been found only in the hands of barbers, peddlers, drovers, rogues, or simple people of the villages and the countryside.

Having suggested to Segovia this idea of drawing on such material, which he happily accepted, I began to write a 'suite', in which, paralleling the form of the 'concerto', the guitar would, nevertheless, still be the virtually complete protagonist.

My last and greatest satisfaction is to think that if Gaspar Sanz could see the score, he would exclaim: 'it's not mine, but I recognise myself in it.'

The *gentilhombre* of the title is Gaspar Sanz himself, and it is to him that the work is dedicated. Nevertheless, I have also referred to Segovia as the 'gentilhombre' of the Spanish guitar, rightly ennobled amongst guitarists and Spanish musicians, and I have paid homage to Andrés Segovia by also dedicating this work to him.

II

The work was composed in the autumn of 1954 and first performed by Segovia in San Francisco in March 1958. All of its themes, except for some short episodes in the last movement, and a considerable amount of the harmonic details, have come from the work of Gaspar Sanz – the guitarist of Philip IV and more especially his son, Don Juan de Austria – a musician in whom the guitar is ennobled, assuming the forgotten sceptre of the old vihuela.

Musical taste had changed a great deal in the years between the reigns of Philip II and Philip IV, and, in contrast to poetry, music – too easily responsive to popular pressures – had become somewhat plebeian. Following the noble repertoire of *pavanas* and *gallardas* there came the trivial styles of *marizápalos*, *villanos*, *españoletas*, and *canarios*, related more to the noise of theatre corrals than to palace balls.

The dances upon which Gaspar Sanz based these and other pieces, some of them published in 1667, faithfully reflect those tastes and styles, and are therefore short, simple and light. The poor musical quality of these themes, which nevertheless retain the freshness of authenticity, requires the collaborator, if the work is to respond to present-day demands, to assume the role of protagonist, without diminishing or debasing the message he is trying to convey to us.

The *Fantasía* is divided into five movements. The 'Villano' which begins the piece develops as a single theme within the melodic framework familiar from the period. There follows a 'Ricercar' in which I develop the fugue which had been briefly sketched by Gaspar Sanz. The third movement, 'Españoleta', is interrupted by an unusual central episode, which serves as a trio – 'toques de la caballería de Nápoles' – which, like other *toques*, such as that of the 'Reina de Suecia' or the 'Rey de Francia', are included in Sanz's manual. The presence of the 'toques de la caballería de Nápoles' is an obvious allusion to that period in which the kingdom of Naples was closely connected to Spain. The 'Siciliana' and the 'Españoleta', on the other hand, are in fact first cousins. The 'Danza de las hachas', of great rhythmic animation, pits the guitar against the orchestra. And the work ends with a 'Canario', a popular dance of deceptive whimsy.

The small orchestra, made up of strings, piccolo, flute, oboe, clarinet, bassoon, trumpet and two horns, serves to sprinkle the music with those strong, bittersweet harmonies which were so to the taste of the period.

Pavana Real

The music for the ballet *Pavana Real* was written in the spring of this year (1955). Its action is carried by twelve musical numbers, preceded by a brief overture (a *Ricercar* in the form of a 'reveille'). The twelve numbers are arranged in three kinds of distinct expression, making up a large 'ordre', as Couperin might have called it. But these dances do not attempt formal and plastic expression, but rather seek to convey psychological insights, something which, whatever the corporeal beauty of dance in a ballet, should never be absent.

In reality, although the characters included in the brief plot are historical (Doña Germaine de Foix, her husband, the Duke of Calabria, Luis de Milán, Doña Mencía, and even the jesters Gilot and Esterot), the chess-game of their lives is not played out on this board, though the passions and attitudes which they symbolise are – grace and frivolity, serenity and constancy, fidelity in the service of the monarchs, and a fierce comic spirit, all typical of the age.

The score is based on a hypothesis and a reality, the reality being the courtly music which is contained in the book of music for the vihuela composed by Luis de Milán, the first of such books for the instrument, which was published in Valencia in 1535. The hypothesis is of those popular pieces which players performed for people to dance to, together with their joyfulness, in a happy, relaxed and refined court, which, nevertheless, always kept a window wide open to the countryside beyond.

Junto al Generalife

As with *Bajando de la meseta* and *En los trigales*, *Junto al Generalife* forms part of an imaginary 'suite' describing the landscape of Spain. Everyone has heard tell of the marvellous gardens of the Generalife, near the Alhambra – one can speak of the murmur of the perfumed breezes, a distant sound of bells, and the colourful flowers beneath the myrtles. And there the guitar also rests, and dreams.

Música para un jardín

Under this title the composer has brought together four *berceuses*, which lull the four seasons of the year to sleep as they successively transform a garden. All of them, though distinct, are rocked in a cradle-song rhythm, which measures and separates the passing of time.

The four *berceuses* – autumn, winter, spring and summer – are preceded and followed by a brief prelude and postlude, forming a continuous whole, which is heard within the small but colourful confines of a small orchestra, comprising piccolo, flute, oboe, cor anglais, clarinet, horn, trumpet, celesta, harp, xylophone and strings.

The *Berceuse de otoño* is carried upon sustained strings, providing a persistent and unusual backdrop, from which emerges a sad melody on the cor anglais and the oboe, interrupted by the tinkling of the celesta, the sound of a distant bell, and a gentle sigh from the violins' harmonics, the whole of this heard over the constant rhythm of the double basses.

The *Berceuse de invierno* is based on a pedal-point to which the cor anglais lends a gentle pastoral air. On this base a clarinet melody is heard, somewhat like a carol, which is repeated by the celesta and concluded by the violins and the woodwind.

A short passage announces the arrival of spring on the sound of bells, and with a theme of a popular nature, played by the violins.

The *Berceuse de verano* is sung by the 'cellos, a slow, serene melody bathed in the little fountains of the garden and in the slow patterns of the violins. The short bars of the postlude conclude the work with the gentle flight of the flute among string harmonics.

This little Suite was used as illustration for the film of the same name.

El hijo fingido

I always wanted to set a play by Lope de Vega to music, and I therefore accepted enthusiastically the version of a work by this writer which was offered to me by my good friend, Jesús María de Arozamena.

In a short time I wrote a score, which has grown considerably following the collaboration with Victoria Kamhi, who, knowing my way of feeling and composing so well, was able to find new situations to attract one's always unsatisfied musical demands.

I have therefore been able to work on a libretto which is just as I wanted – concise, joyous, at times carefree, and at others having a sad tenderness.

For an orchestral composer, the theatre seems a trap with worrying temptations and terrible difficulties, and although I have undertaken this piece with the experience gained from previous compositions for the theatre and the cinema, this is my first work for the theatre in which the music assumes, one might say, almost the entire responsibility.

My wish is for this music to be seen as part of that line which comes from the light-hearted *opera buffa* of the 18th century, developing then in the gentle smile of Mozart and the mischievous one of Rossini, and which in the 19th century mitigates the sadness of Romanticism, or lights up music with the elegance of our popular traditions.

The music of *El hijo fingido* is based almost exclusively on melody. It is music to be sung, and the score consists of twenty numbers, divided into ballads, duets, trios, a brief *concertante* finale and five instrumental numbers – an overture, a prelude to the second act, for harp and orchestra, and a ballet in three parts. The whole of the first act is based on what we might call 'music of Madrid', to contrast with the lyricism of the second, where the amorous rivalry between mother and daughter breaks out. In the orchestral part I have tried to avoid my usual habits as a composer of symphonic works. Its function is intended simply to enhance the voices, so that these can constantly shine.

In conclusion, I wanted to write clear and direct music, continuing in this way our lyric tradition.

Rodrigo's piano music, discussed and performed by the composer

A lecture given to the Academia Médico-Quirúrgica Española and published in their Anales, *May 1964*

Before anything else I should like to thank Dr Hidalgo for the kind words he has said about my intentions. I am going to try to undertake something very difficult, to be modest in saying a little about my own music, before introducing it to you.

There is clearly a subtle but intimate relationship between medicine and music, the reason for which we do not fully understand. It is perhaps because both have a great deal of magic about them, but it is clear that among the non-artistic, non-musical professions, it is doctors in particular who most favour us with their affection and their understanding. It is very unusual to find a doctor who really does not like music. Doubtless, perhaps, because these men, who live with the reality of human pain, are attracted by that abstract and truly subtle essence which is music – so incorporeal, perhaps the most incorporeal of all the arts – and it is precisely this contrast that attracts them. On the other hand, music – and many of those listening know this better than I – also has, and has always had, curative properties, like magic. The old magicians of antiquity were, as everyone knows, part doctors and part musicians, and they also frequently used music as a therapy – music to calm, music to uplift – and even today music serves for both of these as it did in the past, although it is also true that today with the really excessive abuse which is made of it, music is gradually losing its magical powers for us, because we are dulled by it. It is truly an abuse to hear so much music, even when we do not want to, because on the radio and the television music accompanies us in everything, even the daily news bulletins, even in announcements about what is happening. And we always listen to this music, which is slowly deafening us. Nevertheless, music continues to exert on us, as well as its artistic qualities, that magic which is a curative for so many conditions. It was not unusual to use it in this way, above all as a sedative, and the great magnates, the wealthy in the 17th and 18th centuries, at times used the musicians that they employed like pharmacists, since they made them write music to calm them or to induce sleep.

There is the example of the *Goldberg Variations*, which Bach wrote for a music-loving count who suffered from sleeplessness, and in fact he wrote variations which were able to make not only that music-lover sleepy, but the entire public who listens to them today, and this in spite of their great beauty! But forty-five or fifty minutes of the harpsichord indeed sent our good count to sleep, and made him happy.

I'm not going to speak about all the virtues that this music has. I remember now that there was a Catalan doctor who was very important as far as our national instrument, the guitar, is concerned. It was in fact doctor Amat who introduced this instrument at the end of the 16th century, and on the frontispiece of his manual – since it occurred to him to write a little guitar manual, the first, without doubt, to be printed – he writes 'doctor, and musician when God deigns to improve my lot.' Well now, this doctor Amat wrote his little manual to wrest the guitar from the hands of barbers and blood-letters, who were to some extent doctors too, who in fact dominated or monopolised the small guitar of the period. This manual was so successful that twelve or fifteen editions were published in a very short time, and the guitar began to spread its wings and become known.

We could relate many things concerning the link that there has always been between medicine and music. And passing now to my own modest music for the piano, it may be helpful to say something not exactly about the history of the piano, which would be too much, but to place in context the music you are going to hear.

The piano is in reality an instrument of the last century. It is clear that in the 18th century the piano became known and was played, above all, in the last twenty-five years of the century, but it becomes really important in expressing the emotional needs of musicians in the 19th century, when they find in the piano the ideal instrument, the ideal vehicle, for those emotions. But Spain, for various reasons, had no connections with the instrument during this century, and one can hardly find any music which is worth preserving written for the piano in the first eighty years of the 19th century. It will in fact be Isaac Albéniz, born in 1860, who appears in this final quarter of the 19th century, almost the final decade of it, who begins to write for the piano, at first very timidly, but who later, now in the 20th century, writes his great work – of supreme importance internationally for the piano – his suite *Iberia*.

Spanish piano music, then, begins as a branch of post-Romanticism – nationalism – and is derived from a poetic conception of music, and therefore of the piano itself, since that is what we are talking about.

This tendency, this concept of the poetic, that is to say, of narrative, of the power of evocation, of the picturesque, etc., comes clearly in part from Berlioz, the great French musician, and above all from Liszt. Albéniz was for a time a pupil of Liszt when the aged Liszt lived during the last years of his life in Budapest. From this, and from the pleasure Albéniz felt for those same influences, comes the fact that Spanish piano music evolves under the sign of the poetic, and continues to remain faithful to this poetic and evocative tendency in music. Thus, the music of Spain, arising from its pleasure in popular dance and popular rhythms, is predominantly an evocation of landscape, rhythm and dance. The music of Albéniz begins at first timidly, with a series of little poems, salon music, easy music, music for the young ladies of the time, simple and direct. But as I have already said, in the first years of the century and not long before his death, Albéniz in 1909 produces the great work which raises him to universal significance. Suddenly, with one bound, the 'Spanish piano' produces the suite *Iberia*. But the *Iberia* suite, in its colossal greatness, immediately circumscribes Spanish piano music, that is to say, it surrounds Albéniz's successors with an iron band. This enormous work will be like a barrier, and it will be very difficult for Spanish piano music to escape from the confines of this work of genius.

The piano music which follows, that of Granados, of Turina, and even of Manuel de Falla, tries to escape from this restriction, really without being able to, because the suite *Iberia* constitutes, from that time until today, the richest of canvases written for the Spanish piano. Thus the musicians of my generation faced a difficult problem in writing for the instrument. On one side there was this tremendous suite *Iberia*, and on the other the great French Impressionist piano of Debussy and Ravel, and it was thus very difficult to create for it in a way which would be personal.

I have done what I can to try to avoid that magnificent 'Albéniz piano', and to present piano music opposed to it, so to speak, to set against that music – made enormous by accumulation – a music made from *elimination*, that is to say, much smaller, much clearer, and to

221

some extent inspired by an illustrious keyboard composer, not of the piano exactly, but of the harpsichord – not a Spaniard either but very 'Spanish', since he lived for so very many years in Spain – Domenico Scarlatti.

Inspired to some extent, therefore, by this style of keyboard music, and by the characteristics of the 20th-century instrument, I have tried to write my own pieces for the piano. On the other hand, the piano, like all instruments, and all human things, has to die, has to pass on. Instruments live, develop, have a period of splendour, and then are superceded. They disappear when the expressive needs of the composers of a certain period do not need them any more. Each epoch needs its instruments, which are the vehicles for the creative musical force of the composer; and when the emotional needs or the composers' techniques require it, the vehicle must of necessity vary – that is to say, the vehicle becomes the instrument which carries these needs and techniques and transfers them to the concert hall. It has always happened like this, and we have seen how each epoch has had its instruments, which have varied according to the technique and the ethical and emotional needs of composers. I believe, in fact I said a long time ago – and the passing years have confirmed this – that the piano, this good friend, will disappear as an appropriate vehicle for composers' emotions. It is now very difficult to draw out new dimensions and new accents from the piano, which has been dominant for almost two hundred years in the hands of composers and their imaginations. And the piano is becoming tired, is dying as a creative instrument – though not the actual instrument itself, which will of course live for ever.

This explains the difficulties I mentioned before, those difficulties of the 'Spanish' piano, and the 'French Impressionist' piano of the 20th century, to which are now added the current problems of this instrument, which seems so exhausted, and which has already expressed all its mysteries and all its secrets to us. This is what makes it difficult to write for. I began writing for the piano many years ago, in fact, and throughout my years as a composer I have always approached the instrument with great affection and great devotion, trying to write down simply and authentically what I have felt, and what the piano has allowed me to express.

Cuatro danzas de España

These four dances, which have no clear musical connection, are as distinct as can be, even though they are the work of just one composer, and all of a certain kind. Nevertheless, in form, substance and intention they are very different. They do not form a unity, and although they are published as a group, they can each be considered individually.

The first is a *Danza valenciana*. It is inspired by folkloric tradition, its theme being the well-known *jota* or *fandango* of Valencia, with its 'one' and 'two', mysterious numbers whose significance we are not sure of, but alluding, perhaps, to the steps of the dance, perhaps to the figures which the dancers weave. It is clearly a *fandango*, a dance in three-four time, very colourful, popular and picturesque. The piano, of course, takes away this colour and makes it less picturesque, since the instrumental attire of popular music is highly characteristic, with its trombones, guitars, castanets, etc.; and there is also the singer, since this is a dance which is both danced and sung. On the other hand, the piano gives it an artistic dimension, a formal and rather more elevated aesthetic status, rather like a concerto. So, the theme comes from this dance. As for the form of what we are about to hear, it is what we call 'A-B-A', that is to say, it is in three sections, the third of which repeats the first, with a second part, or trio, which is slower and somewhat reminiscent of the refrain of the Valencian *fandango* or *jota*.

The second of these *Cuatro danzas* is a great contrast to the first. The first is very closely linked to popular traditions. This second piece, on the other hand, *Plegaria de la Infanta de Castilla*, makes no allusion at all to any kind of folkloric tradition. It is clearly an evocation of an imagined mediaeval religious dance, but without popular references, nor any melodic element which might bring to mind any popular dance or song, whether mediaeval or not. It is much longer than the first piece, and is written in a rather more challenging form. Everything is linked to the initial idea and is a melodic development of this theme, which continues throughout the dance. At times there is a certain dramatic colouring, an obvious sense of anxiety in the dance, which develops at first very slowly, quietly and calmly, and always within a mediaeval character, with unusual harmonies. This is music of the past, suggesting a possible music from the Middle Ages, but with, of course, the expressive and harmonic recourses of our own time.

Continuing, then, with the contrasts of which I have already spoken, the following dance, *Fandango del ventorrillo*, is again very different, extremely short, and in contrast to the intended harmonic richness of the previous dance, it has a plain and unadorned texture, just a two-voice sketch, very brief, very pared-down, and very difficult.

The fourth dance, *Caleseras*, is a homage to Chueca, as the title and the dedication make clear. This marks the start, I believe – at least in my own music – of a tendency which I myself have called '*neocasticista*'. This is the attempt to approximate to the 'género chico', the *zarzuela*, the closest musical form to the people of Spain, and especially to the people of Madrid, which is certainly the most authentic. To try, therefore, to insert into our symphonic traditions something of the popular – even common – essence of that musical form. I have called this '*neocasticismo*', as opposed to the 'neoclassicism' found in Europe in the 1930s and 1940s. We cannot ourselves be categorised, and we cannot attempt to create a 'neoclassicism', since we have never had 'classical' music in Spain. But we can indeed perhaps attempt to be '*neocasticistas*', (since we cannot be 'neoclassicists'), taking as our inspiration the music of the 19th and 20th centuries. A number of works of mine have been written with this inspiration, together with some of my concertos: the *Concierto serenata* for harp and orchestra, for example, and even the *Concierto de Aranjuez*.

This dance, therefore, is dedicated to Chueca, since it is in part inspired by a brief melodic phrase from one of his *zarzuelas*, and alludes in particular to *Agua, azucarillos y aguardiente*. You will remember in it that argument between the two water-sellers, with the chorus as judge, where you hear: 'They say that Manuela is looking for a fight, but I am perfectly happy where I am – I'm not looking for trouble!', to which the chorus replies: 'She's in the right!' Well, the dance is inspired by those four notes, F, E, D and C. *Caleseras* is just these four notes, F, E, D and C. 'Caleseras' can mean anything – we can take it as referring to those ladies riding in a chaise, whom the composer imagines going off to a bullfight this very afternoon!

Himno de los neófitos de Qumrán
Commentary by Joaquín Rodrigo

The première of this work, commissioned by the fourth Cuenca Week of Religious Music, took place on Holy Thursday, 15th April 1965. The work is scored for three sopranos, men's chorus, and an orchestra consisting of strings (without violins), two flutes, celesta, vibraphone, timpani and percussion.

The music of this hymn is based on a scale formed of nine notes, the first symbolic number, B, F, A, C, D, E, F, G and C, although the composer is not bound by the symbolism suggested by the text. This, in a very special and unexpected way, leads to the final cadence, on a chord of A major, or a *tierce de picardie*, as the French baroque masters would have called it – although I am happy to say that this work has nothing of that style about it. As a result, there is no place here for any Gregorian or Ambrosian influence, which would in any case have made impossible the Psalm's beautiful, and eternal, invocation.

The second symbol is to be heard in the delicate repeated notes uttered by the celesta: D, F, G, D, B flat, F, E, C. And, finally, the third of the symbols is the prayer to the three Archangels, symbolised by the three soprano voices, who hover above, protecting by reason of their divine nature the men's chorus, those disciples of Qumran – ascetics, sages and tenacious watchers of the stars and the sky, so eternally mysterious to mankind.

To conclude, the orchestra is treated with the greatest restraint, reduced to the minimum possible for this poetry, which is so laden with symbols. The percussion is deployed not for its bell-like sounds, but at times in an expressive way, as in the case of the vibraphone, which is used here in a virtually symbolic role. I wanted to associate myself with this beautiful hymn; and I can assert that my humble music is nothing more than this – Franciscan humility in the presence of the beauty of this psalm of the disciples of Qumran.

Himno de los neófitos de Qumrán
Commentary by Victoria Kamhi

A few kilometres to the south of Jericho, near the ancient ruins of Khibet Qumran in the Judean desert, the young shepherd boy, Mohammed Adh-Dib, a Bedouin of the tribe of Ta'Amireh, climbing after a goat that had been lost among the crags of Djebel, discovered in a narrow cave the jars which contained the famous Dead Sea Scrolls.

Since 1947, the date of their discovery, 'the greatest in modern times', as Lankester Harding affirms, these ancient rolls of parchment have caused veritable oceans of ink to be spilled around the world. Archeologists, theologians, paleographers, philosophers and poets have discussed, disputed and even almost come to blows with one another. Today, fifteen years later, the storm has abated, and these rolls, of incalculable value, are resting at last in the temperature-controlled rooms of the Jerusalem Museum.

Among the seven rolls discovered in the first of the Qumran caves (many more would be found later on in caves nearby), they also found, in addition to the very ancient *Book of Isaiah* and the *Commentary of Habbakuk*, a collection of *Psalms of Thanksgiving*, together with *The Book of the Law,* also called the *Manual of Discipline.* This last book ends with the extremely beautiful psalm which Theodor Gaster has called 'Hymn of the Disciples of Qumran', the first verse of which was chosen by Joaquín Rodrigo for his composition of the same name.

Who might the inspired author of this strange poem have been? What we know today for certain is that he belonged to the Qumran sect. This was probably formed just before the reign of John Hircanus (135–104 BC), and died out shortly before the destruction of the Temple in Jerusalem (70 AD). Its origins date back to a schism among the priests in Jerusalem, after the coming to power of Alexander Jannaeus, the king-priest of Judea (103–76 BC). A group of priests, faithful adherents to the ancient Law, refused to recognise as their supreme priest a warrior king whose guilty hands were stained with blood. These pious men, called 'hassidim', preferred to retreat to the desert, where they elected as the supreme priest of Israel the one to whom they gave the title the 'Law-giver'. Beside the Dead Sea they built a monastery where they founded a small community of sages and ascetic philosophers, united there to dedicate their lives to praising God and to penitence. They kept vigil for much of the night in order to fervently pray, and to study the mysteries of the vault of heaven, and the movement of the stars, observing faithfully the precepts of the 'New Alliance'.

From the *Commentary of Habbakuk* we learn that the seond Law-giver, whose strong personality can be sensed from the manuscripts, was taken from his refuge on the 'Day of Atonement' by Alexander Jannaeus himself, who condemned him to be crucified, handing him over to his mercenaries, together with all the others who would not recognise his authority. (According to Dupont-Sommer, this amounted to some six thousand people). The writers of the commentaries tell us that this cruel punishment, which was used in the Roman empire, was imposed for the first time in Israel, on this very occasion, by the cruel tyrant. (*Commentary of Habbakuk*).

Might there not be found amongst these martyrs for their faith the anonymous author of the 'Hymn of the disciples of Qumran', in whose ancient verses there is already reflected, together with the love of God as Creator of the world, with all its natural wonders, that profound lyrical beauty and those mystical elements which we will find again, many centuries later, in the poetry of San Juan de la Cruz and Fray Luis de León?

Joaquín Rodrigo wrote the first of the *Himnos* for the 1965 Festival at Cuenca, for which this programme note was written by the composer and his wife. He later added two more psalm settings, completing the whole work, *Himnos de los neófitos de Qumrán*, in 1974.

Adagio
para orquesta de instrumentos de viento

This work was commissioned from Joaquín Rodrigo for the Pittsburgh Music Festival and was premièred in June 1966, conducted by Robert Austin Boudreau.

In its construction this *Adagio* follows sonata form, without development, that is to say, it has two themes which follow one another in different keys, and which are repeated in the same tonalities. The first theme, of a gentle nature, is entrusted to the melancholy voice of the flute, initially solo, and then lightly accompanied. This theme, which develops through successive modulations, gives way to a second theme of a tormented nature, whose emotion is gradually increased through numerous instrumental figurations. A brief interruption by the brass separates the exposition from the recapitulation of the two themes, ending with a memory of the first theme, bringing the *Adagio* to a pianissimo close.

The two themes of this work are of undeniably Spanish character, although they are the composer's own inventions, and their unusual modalities give them the melodic character typical of Joaquín Rodrigo's music. The harmonic texture is based on the diatonic, but the use of superimposed fourths and fifths frequently gives the work a disturbing vagueness.

Atardecer

This work is intended to enrich the repertoire of piano music for four hands, which is not very extensive. It is the third work written for this combination by Joaquín Rodrigo, the first being the *Gran Marcha de los Subsecretarios*, dedicated to Jesús Rubio – who became a minister – and Antonio Tovar, the famous philologist. Both were excellent pianists. The second work, *Sonatina para dos muñecas*, is dedicated to the composer's granddaughters, as they were beginning their study of the piano. This third work was written not long afterwards and then changed a little in certain ways, but without its original form being altered.

It begins with the presentation of the main theme, consisting of seven notes, which has an unequivocally elegiac character, leading us towards a gentle sunset. Little by little the writing is enriched by a profusion of pianistic effects of considerable brilliance, until it reaches a final 'allegro', but without the work's general character being changed. The piece is full of pianistic effects typical of the composer.

Concierto madrigal

The *Concierto madrigal* for two guitars and orchestra was premièred in 1970 in the vast Hollywood Bowl of Los Angeles by the famous Orchestra of that city, conducted by Rafael Frübeck de Burgos, with Ángel and Pepe Romero as soloists. The work, which had been anticipated with great interest, was greeted with enthusiasm, a response which was repeated afterwards in many US cities.

The *Concierto madrigal*, as suggested by its title, is based on the style and rhythms of an anonymous Renaissance madrigal, *O felici occhi miei*, which begins: 'O happy eyes of mine, which saw in your eyes, lady, such goodness.'* In certain parts, therefore, it takes on a flavour which is somewhat archaic and modal. In others, the melody, which is the main thread of the work, is presented in a more popular style. I have used the episodic structure with a clear intention, since this Concerto departs fundamentally from the usual form. In spite of the established dialogue, and the 'concertante' writing which is adopted, it is more like a 'suite', even though the essential underlying element is the 'variation'. Each of these 'variations' or episodes is described with a title which suggests its mood or scenario, a lightly poetic note which colours the whole score.

The sequence of titles is as follows: 'Fanfarre', 'Madrigal', Entrada', 'Pastorcico, tú que vienes', Girardilla', 'Pastoral', 'Fandango', 'Arieta', 'Zapateado', 'Caccia a la española'. The orchestra consists of piccolo, flute, oboe, clarinet, bassoon, horn, trumpet and strings.

*The madrigal, 'O felici occhi miei', is in fact by Jacques Arcadelt (c 1505 – 1568), though Rodrigo was probably familiar with the melody from the well-known 'glosa' by Diego Ortiz (c 1510 – c 1570).

Invocación y danza

A few days ago, in the newspaper *Ya*, I wrote a brief piece about the brilliant trajectory of the guitar nowadays, recalling at the same time some details about my first composition for the instrument, the *Zarabanda lejana*, written as long ago as 1926. Today, at the request of some friends, I will write something about my latest composition, once again for the guitar, and written some thirty-five years after the former piece. This brief article is not in fact inopportune, since, if not the work, at least its recreation, had as its setting our own 'villa', Villajoyosa.

Exactly a year ago the French musicologist Robert Vidal passed this way on his annual pilgrimage through Spain, looking for me. He is someone, in his position in French radio and television, absolutely devoted to the guitar. Here in our pleasant garden we got to know each other over a beer or two, and he told us of his cherished and already well-advanced project to organise an international competition to award a prize for a new work for the guitar. For two or three years Radiodiffusion-Télévision Française had been organising, at Vidal's suggestion, an international competition for performers, but in 1961 it was to be for composers. It seemed to me an excellent idea, but I was not quite so enthused by Robert Vidal's suggestion, and indeed insistence, that I myself should take part in the competition. But who denies anyone anything in summer, sitting under lemon trees, a few steps from the beach! But privately I had decided not to take part.

Nevertheless, I *did* take part in the competition. That was due to Vicky, my wife, who reminded me when we were back in Madrid that an almost complete sketch of a work for guitar had been lying in a drawer for some time. I had completely forgotten it, in fact; other works and other projects had supplanted it, and it had finally been buried amongst other papers.

I have never enjoyed revising a work of mine. Its themes, its writing, its problems belong to another time, and trying to give life back to all that is almost as hopeless as to desire to relive the past, that beautiful chimera for mankind. But I *did* revise the work. It had been conceived on a veritable plethora of allusions to the music of Manuel de Falla. That sustained its mood and sound-world, in a kind of distance from Falla's own personality, and although the actual themes of the work

231

were my own, in this way a certain magic enveloped, and tempered, my own way of writing. The work, entitled *Invocación y danza* (*Homenaje a Manuel de Falla*), satisfied me – why not say so? Only a little retouching was necessary here and there, and its duration, of six to eight minutes, was ideal. It was, therefore, just right for the competition.

Under the pseudonym of 'Myo Cid' (whenever I am asked the reason for choosing that name, I reply that it is because the Cid's name was 'Rodrigo'), the piece was sent to Paris, and a few weeks later it was awarded the first prize from among the thirty-seven works presented. The concert, in the hands of that wonderful guitarist, Alirio Díaz, took place before a small but well-informed audience, which filled the Salle Gaveau.

What is *Invocación y danza*, and what is it like? Its title, and what I have already written about it, makes that clear. The work opens with a succession of individual harmonics, played one after another, which place the listener, immediately, in a mood of magic, or incantation. The allusions to the music of Falla appear in this way, sustained on a harmonic web of their own, but still within the master's Andalusian impressionism. Then, without a pause, the main theme is heard, but sustained on a clear rhythmic base.

The harmonic language rests upon chords of a ninth and on additional notes which escape from the key of F minor in which the dance is played. Tremolos on the guitar, discords and strumming continue the incorporation of elements of the flamenco guitar into the world of the classical guitar, which the latter absorbs very easily.

The work ends on the first notes of *El amor brujo*, but with very 'Rodrigo harmonies', as one interpreter remarked.

That is all, my friends, that needs to be said. Villajoyosa is once again in some way the inspirer of my music, and I hope that it will go on inspiring it. The quiet of this little house is very suited to it, as is the peace created by this sunlit and tranquil countryside.

Cantos de amor y de guerra

This collection of five songs was commissioned from the composer by the Spanish Radio-Television Orchestra. They form a cycle inspired by ballads, the themes of which are love or the frontier wars with the Moors.

The music and the texts, which have been adapted by Victoria Kamhi, are taken from 16th-century *Cancioneros*. The music of the ballads has been generally slightly modified, with the exception of the fourth, 'Sobre Baza estaba el Rey', which is an original composition.

The composer has endeavoured to keep the atmosphere of these ballads, dressing them in simple harmonies and discreet orchestration. The strings, for example, are only used in two of them: 'Paseábase el Rey moro' and '¡A las armas, moriscotes!' The third, '¡Ay luna que reluces!', is just for voice and flute. In the fourth, 'Sobre Baza estaba el Rey', already referred to, there are flutes, oboes, horn, trumpet and harp, while in the final song, 'Pastorcico tú que has vuelto', only the brass and percussion are used. These limited resources, both harmonic and instrumental, have been employed so that the melody of the ballads is brought out, contributing to the strange atmosphere of that music, which would originally have been accompanied by a vihuela or a small group of instruments. The harmonies are new, nevertheless, as is the overall conception of this music, which is distinguished by its sobriety.

Con Antonio Machado

This collection of ten songs was written in homage to Antonio Machado. They were written in 1971 on texts by this admirable poet, and were first performed on the 4th October 1971 by the soprano María Orán, accompanied on the piano by Miguel Zanetti. The concert took place within the third 'Decade of Music' in Seville, in the Charles V room of the Reales Alcázares. They arose from a commission by the Comisaría General de la Música, as a homage to Joaquín Turina. They are dedicated 'To Victoria'.

Only three of the ten titles of this collection are by Machado himself; 'Preludio', 'Los sueños', and 'Canción del Duero', since Machado normally only numbered his poems. Therefore, to give the other seven songs titles, I have resorted to the usual practice of taking the first words of the poem, or of taking some others which are significant to the sense or idea of the poetry. The songs do not form a cycle like Schubert's *Die schöne Müllerin*, or Schumann's *Dichterliebe*, because I have not found in the complete poetry of Machado a group of poems alluding to one person, or to a continuous sentiment.

Antonio Machado was the poet of Castile, and of his own heart. He loved to sing of the blue mountains and snows of Soria, the green pine-trees, the brown holm-oaks, and the high Duero. He sang repeatedly of roses and sweet April evenings, and of the beloved, with her child-like voice, whom death tore from him so swiftly and so silently.

The poems of Antonio Machado are short and concentrated, and, because many things are left within the shadows of his feelings, they are well suited to music.

I continue to believe in melody, where song is concerned - in the entire, measured musical phrase - and therefore this collection follows this way of composing, from which I have never deviated.

Elogio de la guitarra

My intention was to demand from the player a precise and infallible technique, as well as a deep sensitivity towards the intricately woven themes of the music. I have composed this work as a challenge to the guitarist, basing myself very happily on sonata form.

The first movement, 'Allegro', consists of two halves. The first is a chordal progression, decorated with thirds and scale passages. It leads to a melodic theme which is combined at the end of the movement with chordal writing.

The second movement, 'Andantino', has a more serene character and is an evocation of an ancient Castilian cathedral. The firm sounds of the harmonic chords underline the two themes of a distant plainsong melody. The first of the melodies ends with a tranquil succession of chords which leads in arpeggios to the second theme. These chords help to establish the essence of the theme. The second movement dissolves in the guitar's harmonic register.

The third movement, 'Allegro', begins with animated figures in thirds and develops in extensive scale passages, resembling those heard in the first movement. The second part, marked 'più allegro', is characterised by its rapid outlines, which require great virtuosity, leading to a conclusion of sharp contrasts, with notes played by the left hand being repeated by the player striking the wood of the guitar with his right.

A la busca del más allá

This work was written for the Houston Symphony Orchestra, and to commemorate the bicentenary of the independence of the United States. The score was finished in Madrid in the spring of 1976.

This work can be classified as a symphonic poem, but of a markedly abstract nature, though this is, in fact, only as suggested by the title, since the music has no definitively descriptive content, as is usually the case with works of this nature.

A great stroke on the tam-tam opens and closes the work, fading into the distance, the intention being to evoke in the listener a sensation of mystery and distance, 'the beyond'. By way of introduction, the orchestra presents within a limited timescale two themes which are frequently repeated throughout the work – melodic elements, interrupted at times by brief, rapid episodes.

The orchestral score is in general very clear, apart from those turbulent passages into which a certain level of complexity is introduced by way of atonal effects. The composer uses the full orchestra, although there are sections where only a small combination of instruments is employed, one of them being the flute, harp, xylophone and celesta.

The work ends pianissimo, like a point lost in space – in 'the beyond'.

Concierto pastoral

This Concerto was composed in response to a commission by the outstanding flautist James Galway, and was premièred in London in October 1978.

The work is divided into three movements, the first being in classical form with first and second subjects. It presents the soloist with extraordinary difficulties in the rapid figuration of the first theme, and the constant successions of fourths, which traverse the entire length of the instrument in arpeggios. The second subject has a more pastoral character, one might say in a popular Valencian style, and contrasts with the headlong progress of the first subject.

The second movement is an 'Adagio', interrupted by a brief 'scherzo'. It is composed of three themes, the first nostalgic, with light decorations; the second, brief and fast-moving, with pipe-like details; and the third, more restful. The cadenza, which is habitual in this musical form, occurs in this movement.

The third movement is a rondo in the style of a rustic dance, in which the refrain, joyous and lively, alternates with more restrained and melodic sections.

The orchestra is reduced to a minimum as far as the wind section is concerned – flute, oboe, clarinet, horn and trumpet. The key of the work is D major.

Concierto como un divertimento

This Concerto, dedicated to Julian Lloyd Webber, was composed in the first months of 1981. Lloyd Webber had asked me for a work which would sound 'Spanish', not a difficult thing for a Spanish composer to accomplish, and also that it should be accessible for the public. This gave rise to the idea that it should be a 'Concierto como un divertimento'.

The first movement opens with a rhythmic formula in which the 'cello plays pizzicato, having a certain *bolero* flavour. Although it is in five sections, this rhythmic formula becomes ever more important throughout the movement. There follows a *sevillanas* theme, and a third, in the rhythm of a *seguidilla*. Neither of these two themes is developed in the customary way, but both reappear in different keys, the movement ending with a reappearance of the opening rhythm.

The second movement is inspired by an old Castilian ballad, 'Ya se sienta el rey Ramiro'. It is slow-moving, but is interrupted by a faster episode and by the soloist's cadenza, based on music from the first movement, which in turn gives way to the 'lento' with which this second movement began.

The third movement is written in sonata form, with a 'scherzando' principal theme, and a second which is more 'cantabile' and impassioned.

The orchestration of the Concerto is made up of two flutes, two oboes, two clarinets, two horns, two trumpets, and strings. The work is in the key of G major.

Concierto para una fiesta

The *Concierto para una fiesta* is the first concerto for solo guitar and orchestra composed by Joaquín Rodrigo since the universally popular *Concierto de Aranjuez*, written in 1939. It was commissioned in 1982 by William and Carol McKay, of Fort Worth in Texas, to celebrate the coming-out into society of their daughters Alden and Lauri – hence its title. It was premièred in private on that occasion, on the 5th March 1983, played by Pepe Romero and the Fort Worth Chamber Orchestra, conducted by John Giordano.

The new Concerto is an incontestably Spanish work, and uncompromising in the severe technical demands it makes on the guitarist. In fact, Pepe Romero had no hesitation in describing it as the most difficult work he had ever played.

Two themes dominate the first movement, original but of a marked Valencian character. The soloist and the orchestra share the exposition of the first, in A minor. The second ('poco più lento'), in D major, unfolds above a sustained 'A' on the horn, which seems to evoke the spirit of El Cid and the Moorish past of Valencia. The atmosphere is heightened with fragments of scales played by the woodwind, reminiscent of *Schéhérezade*, and which in the second movement become important thematically. After a demanding transition passage, the guitar leads the orchestra back to the first theme, before launching into the written cadenza.

Although the cor anglais plays a significant part in the main theme of the introverted second movement, it would be a mistake to look for or even, forty years on, to expect another theme like that of *Aranjuez*. In fact, in spite of its form, this movement is the antithesis of its world-famous predecessor. Its principal basis is rhythm rather than melody. Here there is nothing of the rhythmic serenity of the preceeding work. By contrast, there is a constant alternation between two bars of 6/8 with one bar of 5/8, and this is complicated by different groupings within the two patterns (2x3 and 3x2 in the 6/8 bars, and 2+3 in the 5/8). The result is a continuous, agitated and almost anguished flow throughout the movement, until, at the heart of the cadenza, which is also written out, a form of peaceful 3/4 andante rhythm is achieved. The initial theme is then heard again on the clarinet, beneath the changing colours of the strings, leading to a magical resolution.

By contrast, the rondo finale, where the percussion makes its first appearance, is both extrovert and appropriate to the mood of a celebration, with a *sevillana* as its recurring principal theme. Two secondary themes appear, one of them in the woodwind and brass, which skip through the sections of the movement with a freedom which recalls Stravinsky's *Circus Polka*.

Cántico de San Francisco de Asís
Alabanza de las criaturas

In 1982 I received a visit from Father Merino, a Franciscan friar whom I didn't know. He was middle-aged, very affable and charming. He was accompanied by a famous aviator, a friend of the Convent, whose name escapes me. The visitors told me that in that very year they were celebrating the 800th anniversary of the birth of St Francis of Assisi, and they suggested that I should write a choral work on the Saint's wonderful poem, 'All-highest, omnipotent good Lord', from the book *The Little Flowers of St Francis*. I told them that I had always been drawn to the Saint, as had my wife Victoria, and that we had read the book many years before in Paris, but had since mislaid it. Father Merino kindly offered us the book he had brought with him, with a marker showing where the poem was which he wished set to music.

I was very attracted by the idea of dedicating a work to St Francis of Assisi, the great friend of animals and of nature. I began work immediately, and a few months later the *Cántico de San Francisco* was finished. This poem, which is virtually the beginning of Italian literature, was composed some months before the Saint's death, when he was ill and almost blind, in the convent of San Damiano in Assisi. Nevertheless it joyously celebrates the work of God who made the universe and its creatures.

This was not the first time that the figure of St Francis of Assisi had inspired a work of mine. In 1936 I composed the *Triptic de Mossèn Cinto* on three poems by Jacint Verdaguer, entitled 'The Sacred Harp', 'St Francis's Violin', and 'St Francis and the Grasshopper'. Neither was it the first time I had written a cantata. In 1953, commissioned by the University of Salamanca, where it was first performed, I wrote *Música para un códice salmantino*, based on the 'Ode to Salamanca' by Miguel de Unamuno.

As far as the composition of the *Cántico de San Francisco* is concerned, I can say that it did not cause me too much difficulty. It seemed as if the Saint was inspiring me. In this sublime poem all of nature is present, as I sense it. It is evoked with all its splendour, all its beauty, all its joy and all its sadness. There is brother sun, with his burning rays, sister moon with her melancholy light, the green and leafy woods, the joyful lark, whose song ascends to heaven, the timid deer, the squirrel gliding along the branches to gather the juicy pinenuts on which it feeds...

In the *Cántico de San Francisco* I wanted to capture in my music those verses of the Saint, simply and serenely. I use the power of the full orchestra only rarely, to illustrate certain moments in the text, and for the praise of the final pages. Magical passages for the flute give an oriental feeling to certain parts of the work, suggesting at the same time visions of the 'eternal Jerusalem' to which the Christian soul aspires. The world première took place in London on the 15th March 1986, performed by the The Renaissance Choir and the Bournemouth Sinfonietta, conducted by Raymond Calcraft, to whom the work is dedicated. The work was first heard in Spain, in Madrid on the 18th April 1990, and in Barcelona on the 20th, given by the same orchestra and conductor, with Catalan choirs.

Concerning the Creation of Music

There is nothing more shadowy or more hidden in impenetrable mystery than the process of musical creation. Where does this capacity come from, which one would say is innate, of 'inventing' melodies (as our *vihuelistas* used to say), discovering harmonies lying within strings or in the open tubes of wind instruments, and of creating structures in sound? For years, for centuries, man has tried to discover this mystery and to explain this subtle and complicated mechanism, without until now having been able to raise other than an edifice of haphazard and pedantic hypotheses. This musical capacity has undoubtedly been something instinctive, although with the passage of time, study and other circumstances may have enlivened and developed that latent faculty.

From the beginnings of man's existence he has been surrounded by the strange, constant and magical music of nature, which excites or calms him, which fills him with terror or happiness. The sound of the sea or of running streams, the whisper of leaves moved by the wind ('bells through the leaves', Debussy called it), the crash of thunder, the gallop of hooves, or the song of birds, have been able to influence man's musical potential, gifted as he is with a power of imitation. But also, and particularly, that unknown and essential musical faculty to which I alluded before, and which has served to express his feelings and emotions, such as his joy or his sadness, by means of sound.

A product of thousands of years, and a faithful manifestation of the most diverse cultures, we have before us today the most subtle and complicated artistic language, always in ferment and subject to constant evolution and transformation. We know the power of music to fire the spirit, relieve tiredness, dull the senses, awaken love, and enhance pleasure or increase sadness; we also know of its external mechanics. But we know little of its hidden essence.

The composer stands absorbed and astonished before his own creation. He is able to analyse its structure, but in what does his creative function consist? He knows that music is sufficient not only unto itself: it also portrays and exalts the emotion of words, evokes in us a past feeling or happening, is capable of describing or even narrating an event, or of imitating a natural phenomenon, and he knows how its vast technique has been gradually developed over the centuries. From the rudimentary and rough clapping of hands and stamping of feet, from the primitive beating and rolling of drums, from the incipient singing of his voice, or the rough, sharp sound of his rustic horns, man goes on to discover the tinkling of stringed instruments, the soft sound of the flute or the war-like calls of bugles. He discovers – and this is one of his most unexpected achievements – the ability to express himself musically in different and multiple forms. He obtains a rhythmic variety that is virtually infinite, develops a sense of hearing which understands and assimilates an even greater number of sounds, supports ever renewed harmonic clusters, and retains and transmits a whole structure of sound which passes before him and which lives only in time. What magic alchemy music distils!

In antiquity divine origins were ascribed to music, and one of the nine muses, Euterpe, was endowed with musical attributes. We ourselves visualise God on His throne surrounded by legions of angels and seraphim, who sing His praises to all eternity. The first doctors were also musicians, and the musicians were wise men who with their magic and their music cured the sick and predisposed them to obtain the favour of the gods. These practices have come down to our own times, and one can still see dervishes put snakes to sleep with the sound of their flutes, while they ceaselessly twist and turn. And, as in centuries long ago, music is recognised as having curative powers, not only to placate and mitigate our passions but also serving to cure other ills. The priests when they addressed their gods or implored their favours, did so, and still do, by chanting and singing; and it was by singing that they transmitted to their people the predictions of the oracles. They sang, and sing, their prayers in order that their words may go higher, to the heights, since music is an art with neither weight nor specific measure. Thus Mendelssohn was able to write 'On wings of song'. And it is wonderful that Saint Augustine has told us that on the Day of Judgement our bodies will become sound, that is to say something ethereal, intangible, like our spirit.

Divinity and magic surround the essence and origin of music, and our 16th-century masters, as I said before, called themselves 'inventors', and took as their example Orpheus, that demi-god who calmed the anger of the furies with his song, and was able to tear from their grasp his beloved Euridice.

We have tried to harness and encapsulate the gift of creation, teaching it through fixed rules and trusted methods; but the only thing we can learn and teach – and even this varies over time – is what man has been able to codify. We learn the delicate and subtle mathematics of musical metre; we know how to order the steps of the various tonal functions and their hierarchy within the diatonic system, in which our art has remained during so many years; we understand and recognise the distinct forms and structures which those same tonal hierarchies and the power of metre have engendered; and we recognise thematic antagonisms, their implications and consequences, the variety of agents of sound, which cause in our emotions such differing sensations. All of this we practise and learn, but in what does musical creation itself consist, and where does it reside? What is inspiration and in what hidden recess of our being can it be found, even if at times it seems to come to us as a result of a powerful effort of will?

We create, but I think that we do not know what creation consists of, even though we may know at times the origin of the causes which motivated it. It is for philosophers and researchers into the subject of aesthetics to unravel the mystery and the why and wherefore of artistic creation. Let there remain for us composers the miracle of ordering new harmonic progressions, discovering neologisms in sound, singing a new melody, or making vibrate a previously unheard web of orchestral sounds.

I believe, finally, that we have a musical gift because God has given us a tiny spark, a momentary flash from his immense and depthless creative power. The only thing which we must do is to proffer it, and share it, with true modesty and infinite humility.

*Musica laetitiae comes
medicina dolorum*

('Music is the companion of joy
and a remedy for suffering')

Inscription on the lid of a virginal in
The Music Lesson
(1662-65)
by Jan Vermeer

Appendices

Personalia

Albéniz, Isaac, 1860-1909, Spanish pianist and composer.

Alonso, Odón, 1925-2011, Spanish composer and conductor.

Amengual, René, 1911-1954, Chilean composer and pianist.

Arámbarri, Jesús, 1902-1960, conductor and composer.

Argenta, Ataúlfo, 1913-1958, Spanish conductor.

Arozamena, Jesús María, 1918-1972, Spanish writer of *zarzuela* libretti.

Backhaus, Wilhelm, 1884-1969, German pianist.

Barbieri, Francisco, 1823-1894, Spanish composer, creator of the *zarzuela*.

Bardi, Giovanni, Conte di Vernio, 1534-1612, founder of the Florentine 'Camerata'.

Böhm, Karl, 1894-1981, Austrian conductor.

Bretón, Tomás, 1850-1923, Spanish conductor and composer of operas and *zarzuelas*.

Bülow, Hans von, 1830-1894, German conductor, composer and pianist.

Caballero, Fernández, 1845-1906, Spanish composer of popular *zarzuelas*.

Caccini, Giulio, 1550-1618, singer and composer, member of the Florentine *Camerata*.

Carissimi, Giacomo, 1605-1674, pioneering Italian composer of oratorio.

Carvajal, Armando, 1893-1972, Chilean composer and conductor.

Casanova, Juan, 1893-1976, Chilean composer and conductor.

Cassadó, Gaspar, 1897-1966, Spanish 'cellist.

Cavalieri, Emilio dei, 1550-1602, Italian composer, choreographer and organist.

Cesti, Antonio, 1623-1669, Italian composer, singer and organist.

Chapí, Ruperto, 1851-1909, Spanish composer of *zarzuelas*, founder of the Sociedad de Autores.

Chueca, Federico, 1846-1908, Spanish composer of *zarzuelas*.

Díaz, Alirio, 1923 – , Venezuelan guitarist.

D'Indy, Vincent, 1851-1931, French composer, teacher and author.

Esplá, Óscar, 1889-1976, Spanish composer.

Fischer, Edwin, 1886-1960, Swiss conductor and pianist.

Forns, José, 1897-1952, Spanish composer.

Fuenllana, Miguel de, c 1500-1579, Spanish composer and arranger of popular songs.

Furtwängler, Wilhelm, 1886-1954, German conductor and composer.

Gesualdo, Prince Carlo, 1560-1613, Italian composer, lute player and, reputedly, murderer.

Gieseking, Walter, 1895-1956, German pianist.

Giménez, Gerónimo, 1854-1923, Spanish *zarauela* composer.

Gluck, Christophe Willibald, 1714-1787, German composer.

Granados, Enrique, 1867-1916, Spanish composer and pianist.

Hálffter, Ernesto, 1905-1989, Spanish composer and conductor, brother of Rodolfo.

Hálffter, Rodolfo, 1900-1987, Spanish composer and brother of Ernesto.

Honegger, Arthur, 1892-1955, Swiss composer.

Hummel, Johann Nepomuk, 1778-1837, Austrian composer.

Imperio, Pastora, 1889-1979, Spanish dancer and film actress.

Kjerulf, Halfdan, 1815-1868, Norwegian composer, admired by Grieg.

Knappertsbusch, Hans, 1888-1965, German conductor.

Krauss, Clemens, 1893-1954, Austrian conductor and opera impresario.

Lamote de Grignón, Ricard, 1899-1962, Catalan composer and conductor.

Landino, Francesco, c 1325-1397, Italian composer and organist.

Lassus, Orlande de, c 1530-1594, Flemish Renaissance composer.

Legrenzi, Giovanni, 1626-1690, Venetian composer of masses, oratorios and operas.

Leng, Alfonso, 1884-1974, Chilean composer of songs and piano works.

Luna, Pablo, 1879-1942, Spanish composer of zarzuelas.

Maeterlinck, Maurice, 1862-1949, Belgian playwright, poet and essayist.

Manrique de Lara, Manuel, 1863-1929, Spanish composer and musicologist.

Menéndez Pidal, Ramón, 1869-1968, Spanish academic and folklorist.

Meyerbeer, Giacomo, 1791-1864, German composer of Romantic operas.

Milán, Luis de, c 1500-c 1561, Spanish composer and *vihuela* player.

Mompou, Frederic, 1893-1987, Spanish composer and pianist.

Morales, Cristóbal de, c 1500-1553, Spanish composer of predominantly sacred music.

Ockeghem, Jean de, c 1410 -1497, Flemish Renaissance composer.

Palestrina, Giovanni Pierluigi da, c 1525-1594, Italian Renaissance composer.

Paungartner, Bernhard, 1887-1971, Austrian conductor, composer and musicologist.

Pedrell, Felipe, 1841-1922, Spanish composer, guitarist, musicologist and teacher.

Pérez Casas, Bartolomé, 1873-1956, Spanish composer and conductor.

Peri, Jacopo, 1561-1633, Italian composer of Baroque opera.

Ponce, Manuel, 1882-1948, Mexican composer and musicologist.

Près, Josquin des, 1450-1521, Flemish Renaissance composer.

Querol, Leopoldo, 1899-1985, Spanish pianist.

Rameau, Jean-Philippe, 1683-1764, French composer and music theorist.

Richter, Hans, 1843-1916, Austrian-Hungarian conductor.

Rinuccini, Ottavio, 1562-1621, Italian poet and opera librettist.

Roland-Manuel, Alexis, 1891-1966, French composer and critic.

Rore, Cipriano de, 1515 or 1516-1565, Franco-Flemish composer.

Salvador, Josefina, 1920-2006, Valencian violinist.

Santa Cruz, Domingo, 1899-1987, Chilean composer.

Sainz de la Maza, Regino, 1896-1981, Spanish guitarist.

Sanz, Gaspar, 1640-1710, Spanish composer, guitarist and organist.

Scarlatti, Domenico, 1685-1757, Italian composer, son of Alessandro.

Scarlatti, Alessandro, 1660-1725, Italian composer.

Segovia, Andrés, 1893-1987, Spanish guitarist.

Sepúlveda, María Luisa, 1898-1958, Chilean composer.

Serrano, José, 1873-1941, Spanish composer of *zarzuelas*.

Simrock, German music publishing house.

Schmitt, Florent, 1870-1958, French composer.

Soler, Antonio, 1729-1783, Spanish cleric and composer.

Sopeña, Federico, 1917-1991, Spanish musicologist and author.

Soro, Enrique, 1884-1954, Chilean composer, pianist and academic.

Sorozábal, Pablo, 1897-1988, Spanish composer of *zarzuelas*.

Spohr, Ludwig/Louis, 1784-1859, German conductor and violinist.

Terán, Tomás, dedicatee of various works by Villa-Lobos.

Toldrá, Eduard, 1895-1962, Spanish composer, conductor and concert violinist.

Victoria, Tomás Luis de, c 1548-1611, Spanish Renaissance composer.

Vives, Amadeo, 1871-1932, Spanish composer of operas and *zarzuelas*.

Willaert, Adrian, 1490-1562, Flemish Renaissance composer.

Wittgenstein, Paul, 1887-1961, Austrian pianist.

Zanetti, Miguel, 1935-2008, Spanish pianist and accompanist.

Glossary

Bolero, Spanish dance in 3/4 time, dating from the 17th century.

Bulerías, Spanish *flamenco* dance in 12 beats.

Canario, Renaissance dance, popular throughout Europe.

Cancioneros, collections of Spanish verse or song-books.

Cantiga, mediaeval Spanish song form.

Costumbrismo, depictions of everyday Spanish life and customs,
     , originating in the 17th century.

Españoleta, Spanish Renaissance dance.

Fandanguillas, lively version of the *fandango*.

Fandango, Spanish dance in 3/4 time.

Fantasía, musical composition, frequently improvised.

Galliard, Renaissance dance.

Género chico, see *zarzuela*.

Jácaras, songs of Arabic origin.

Jota, dance in 3/4 time, originally from Aragón.

Majo/a, flamboyant members of the Spanish lower classes, particularly
     of Madrid, in the 18th and 19th centuries.

Maravedí, gold or silver coin in mediaeval Spain.

Marizápalos, primitive Spanish rustic dance.

Panadero, Spanish rustic dance form similar to the *zapateado*.

Pasapié, rustic dance of French origin ('passepied') of the 17th and
     18th centuries.

Pavana, stately Renaissance dance.

Ricercar, elaborate instrumental composition of the 16th and 17th
     centuries, similar to the motet.

Romanza, ballad in verse or music.

Seguidilla, Spanish song or dance in 3/4 time.

Sevillana, song and dance from Seville, derived from the *seguidilla*.

Tiento, Spanish keyboard composition akin to the *fantasía*.

Verismo, 'realism', associated with Italian Romantic opera.

Vihuela, Spanish string instrument of the Renaissance, forerunner of
     the guitar.

Villano, Spanish rustic dance form.

Zapateado, *flamenco* dance featuring percussive heel stamping.

Zarzuela, Spanish light opera, originating in the 17th century.

Publishers of Joaquín Rodrigo's Music

Joaquín Rodrigo – Catálogo/Catalogue

A complete guide to the composer's music can be obtained from:

EDICIONES JOAQUÍN RODRIGO
General Yagüe, 11 – 4J, 28020 Madrid, Spain
www.joaquin-rodrigo.com, ediciones@joaquin-rodrigo.com

Other publishers

BOOSEY & HAWKES BOTE & BOCK GMBH
Anton J Benjamin GmbH, Lützowufer 26, 10787 Berlin, Germany
www.boosey.com, musikverlag@boosey.com

CHESTER MUSIC LTD
8/9 Frith Street, London W1V 5TZ, UK
www.musicsales.co.uk, music@musicsales.co.uk

G SCHIRMER INC
257 Park Avenue South, 20th floor, New York, NY 10010, USA
www.schirmer.com, schirmer@schirmer.com

SCHOTT & CO LTD
48 Great Marlborough Street, London W1V 2BN, UK
www.schott-music.com, info@schott-music.com

SCHOTT MUSIK GMBH & CO KG
Weihergarten 5, D-55116 Mainz, Germany
www.schott-music.com, info@schott-music.com

UME (UNIÓN MUSICAL EDICIONES SL)
Marqués de la Ensenada 4, 28004 Madrid, Spain
www.musicsales.com, unionmusicalediciones@musicsales.com